D0183280

NOW IS THE TIME

ABOUT THE AUTHOR

SR STANISLAUS KENNEDY is an Irish Sister of Charity and the founder of Focus Ireland, the Inaugural Council of Young Social Innovation Ireland, and the Sanctuary She has been instrumental in developing and implementing social-service programmes that have benefited thousands of needy people throughout Ireland and Europe. For this work, she has received many awards, including Honorary Degrees of Law from Trinity College Dublin, the National University of Ireland, the Open University, as well as a presidential medal from New York University.

She is the author of three best-selling books, *Now Is The Time* (TownHouse, 2006 Hardback) *Gardening the Soul* (Simon & Schuster/TownHouse, 2001) and *Seasons of the Day* (TownHouse, 2003). Her latest book is *Stillness, through my Prayer* (TownHouse, 2006).

NOW IS THE TIME

Spiritual Reflections

Expanded Edition

Sr Stanislaus Kennedy

TOWN
HOUSE
DUBLIN

248

First published in hardback in 1998, by

Town House Dublin
THCH Ltd
Mount Pleasant Business Centre
Mount Pleasant Avenue
Dublin 6
www.townhouse.ie

This edition published 2006

ISBN: 1-86059-250-3
978-1-86059-250-8

1 2 3 4 5 6 7 8 9 10

A CIP catalogue record for this book is available from the British Library

Cover image © Photographer/Getty Images
Cover design by Sin É Design

Printed and Bound in Great Britain by
Cox & Wyman Ltd, Reading, Berkshire

CONTENTS

ACKNOWLEDGEMENTS

Many people have been involved in the writing of this book and I am deeply grateful to them all. I am particularly grateful to Bernice Turner, Julie Sheehan, Jacinta Ralph Kennedy and Síle Wall, who have provided invaluable help with typing and reading the various drafts of the book. I want to extend a very special thanks to Siobhán Parkinson, who edited the book and who encouraged me to write it in the first place.

My association with TownHouse and its staff has been a pleasure and a joy. I greatly appreciate the professionalism, expertise and encouragement of Treasa Coady at all times.

To all those I carry in my heart, named and unnamed, I say thanks.

INTRODUCTION

Our experiences are common to all of us, and yet each experience can only be lived uniquely by each of us. This book is an invitation to appreciate all our experiences. It is an invitation to live in the present moment. It is an invitation to share that living with each other, so that we can understand it before we lose it, enjoy it before we miss it. It is an invitation to realise that this time is our time to live, our only time; this time is now; and it is ours. This is our time to make a difference.

Perhaps most books, especially books like this, have to be lived before they are written, but I make no claim to be living out the full implications of what is written in this book. I have, however, begun the journey. I have chosen this particular path, mainly because of people I have encountered in my life who have been an inspiration to me: people who are steadfastly searching for meaning in their lives; people who live with questions, who embrace wonder and imagination; people who live with struggle and suffering, peace and deep joy.

Such people are sometimes artists, writers, poets, storytellers, lifegivers; sometimes they are members of my family, congregation or community; or they may be friends or colleagues or people I encounter through my work; in particular, they are people who live on the edge, in one way or another. People like this have taught me that life is for living, searching, seeking, loving and striving. They have taught me that we can come out of each moment, each situation, each experience more loving and more beautiful than when we entered it.

There is a season for everything

A time for every occupation under heaven

A time for giving birth

A time for dying...

A time for sowing

A time for reaping...

A time for living...

A time for peace...

from Ecclesiastes 3

A TIME TO LIVE

My life belongs to the whole community and as long as I live it is my privilege to do for it whatsoever I can. Life is a sort of splendid torch that I have got hold of for the moment and I want to make it burn as brightly as possible before handing it over to future generations.

GEORGE BERNARD SHAW

Everything has its time, and that time is always now. The time is always now to live our lives, every minute, every hour, every day, every year. Whatever circumstances we find ourselves in, those are the circumstances we have to live with, now. Now is the time to live the lives we have been gifted with. If we put it off till tomorrow to live, then we have lost today.

Live life to the full

Life is for living but we can miss it and let it pass us by if we are unwilling or unable to engage with it in the present. Life is not a consumer good, a thing to be grasped, held, used. We cannot cage life, we cannot freeze it; it moves on, it races and limps, it changes pace, it reaches highs and sinks to lows; sometimes it is too slow and too sluggish for us, at other times too fast to follow and difficult to bear. It is the most we can do, sometimes, to keep up with it.

The real measure of life is not whether we have lived the length of our days, but whether we have lived the depth and breadth of them – whether, in other words, we have lived them to the full. All the experiences of life – births and deaths, loving and losing, gaining and failing, laughing and crying – happen in every life and we cannot avoid, evade or elude them. We cannot reduce life to our own size. What we can do is explore and drink deep from each moment; accept, acknowledge, rejoice in every experience, some exhilarating, some exhausting, but all of them important; endure every part of the way; learn from every colourless as well as from every colourful moment in our lives.

Life is not what happens outside of us; life is happening inside of us. Life not only happens to us; it happens in us, it happens through us, it happens because of us and in spite of us. Life is lived both through what we bring to it and through what we take from it.

There is no such thing as a meaningless moment or a meaningless life. If we are open to it, life will teach and shape us to become people of wisdom, compassion and joy, in our age, in our time. For that to happen, every small part of life must be lived. If we are open to life, the cycle of time shapes and reshapes our misshapen selves until we become what we are called to be.

grasp the moment

To live life well, we must live the present moment. But it is not easy to be present to the present, because we are constantly told to be looking in front of us. Very often we are not here at all, we only think we are here. We live with one foot in tomorrow: what is coming is seen as more important than the now; what is yet to be got, to be seen, to be achieved, can easily become the all-important thing; and while we wait for it and live with our plans, the present moment, which is very rich within us, is lost. As Brendan Kennelly says, 'How easy it is to maim the moment with expectation, to force it to define itself.'

individualism

Today more than ever before in human history we have the knowledge, the information and the technology to find solutions to problems and control situations in a way that would have been unthinkable in the past. But at the same time, we are becoming more and more individualistic in our pursuit of success. We are taught that nothing must interfere with or take precedence over our personal interests, that we deserve the best for ourselves. But in our rush to compete and achieve, we can easily whiz past the moment and miss the living.

As we become more individualistic, so also we become more and more isolated in our own competitiveness. We move like ships in the night, not touching each other. We form support groups with strangers and yet maybe we don't know our next-door neighbours. In the place of neighbourhood we have people who are vulnerable, isolated and very alone.

Now that we have the best-educated people in the history of the world, we do not know what to do with what we know. Everything is too big, too overwhelming, so we mind our own business, ignoring the homeless, elderly, truly desolate and sick people that are all around us, assuming they are somebody else's responsibility.

our time, right now

In the midst of this fast, competitive, industrialised, consumer-driven world, people are starting to say that this cannot go on. More and more people are asking, What can be done to reverse this trend towards extreme individualism? How can we fill this gap between individualism and community? How can we live our lives, caring for ourselves and being supportive and comforting to others? How can we make a difference in our time?

I believe that we can only fill this gap and make a positive, constructive difference by taking responsibility for our time and our society and by developing a sense of ownership of the world and the times we live in. This is our time and it is up to us to choose our destinies, just as it was the time of Francis in Assisi, Gandhi in India, Thich Nhat Hanh in Vietnam, Martin Luther King in America, Nelson Mandela in South Africa, Pope John XXIII in Rome, John Hume and Mary Robinson in Ireland, and the many other countless people who emerged, against the odds, in their own time.

This is my time right here, right now, in this isolated spot or in this village, in this town, in this city or suburb. What happens here, now, is my responsibility. It is not a matter of doing great things: it is a matter of doing or saying small things with responsibility and courage.

a time to be born

There is indeed a time to be born, to come out of the cocoon of the self, to speak and to act and to take responsibility. The model Christians are given for living our lives is the life of Jesus. He risked everything; he was abandoned, rejected, betrayed and killed for being who he was, for saying, doing what he did in his time; he was crucified for asking the right questions of the right people and for standing up and taking responsibility for the right things in his time. This is what it means to be born to the world, to break what is false and what is hidden and destructive in our time.

It is not easy. There are, however, great spiritual comforts for us if we are all willing to become people of truth in our time, however hard it may be. To live with honesty and integrity, letting go of falsity, gives us a new sense of freedom and truth. Once we have broken through the pretences, the barriers, the falsities that blind us and bind us, we are free, we are free forever and no-one can ever take that freedom from us.

With freedom, truth, honesty and integrity comes self-esteem. Self-esteem is something that once truly acquired we can never lose; as Dag Hammarskjöld said: 'Life only demands from you the strength you possess. Only one feat is possible – not to have run away.'

When we have done what we must do, what we were put here to do at this time, in this place, we are who we are called to be and nobody can take that from us. However hard life may be, however difficult the tests and pressures, even if we appear to fail and people leave us and reject us and disown us, we will never die before we have lived our lives to the full, and even in death we will live on in the minds and hearts of those who follow us.

A TIME TO DIE

Unless the grain of wheat falls to the ground and dies it remains just a grain of wheat, but if it dies, it produces much fruit.

JOHN 12:24

I know – in fact, I am related to – a young family that experienced the tragic death of their treasured little daughter Bláthnaid at the age of eighteen months. The convention of our time is to deny death, to pretend it isn't happening, to sanitise it, to make sure it only happens in hospitals and to hide it in funeral homes. But Bláthnaid's parents defied those conventions and insisted on bringing their daughter home to their house for a wake. In making that choice, they were observing an old Irish tradition. In traditional neighbourhoods, the family, friends and neighbours of a person who was dying spent time with them, maybe speaking to them, maybe in silence, maybe praying together, and after they died, this process continued, people praying in silence or talking to each other, eating and drinking and celebrating the life of the person who had just left them. That tradition of the wake is a recognition of the continuation of life into and beyond death. Bláthnaid's parents were glad of those precious hours with their child, that waking time, with the house full of friends and neighbours and family. When the baby was taken to the church, and from there to the burial place, the family continued to talk to her, and for a long time afterwards both the parents and the other children would talk to Bláthnaid. They would light a candle sometimes, to represent her and as a way of keeping in touch with her, and in that way, the child the family has lost continues to have a presence in that home. Bláthnaid has never left them, and they never left her.

the Irish tradition

In honouring their child like this and in keeping her memory alive in a completely natural way, this family was instinctively acknowledging that death and life are one. Probably without ever thinking about it in those terms, they were taking the idea of eternal life, the idea that death is not the end, absolutely literally.

Not everyone feels able to believe in eternal life, but even those of us who do are very often unable to live our lives day to day with that sort of matter-of-fact conviction. We have spiritualised eternal life in a way that is false. We have distanced it from us. We think spatially, in terms of distance and separations, not in terms of having those who have died still at the centre of our lives.

It has been traditional in Ireland to regard the dead as very close to those who are living. Peig Sayers, a traditional storyteller who lived on the Great Blasket Island off the coast of Kerry (and whom I knew as an old lady when I was a child) was once asked where heaven was. In reply, she said it was just a few inches above the tallest man on the island. Heaven and earth, like life and death, were one in the traditional way of thinking.

Whether or not Peig realised it, her belief about heaven's closeness to earth is very similar to the thinking of the great medieval mystic known as Meister Eckhart. When he was asked where does the soul of a person go after death, Eckhart said, 'No place. Where else would the soul be going, where else is the eternal world? It can be nowhere other than here.' We have somehow managed to lose that sense of the nearness of eternity and to forget that once the soul is free of the body, time and space, distance and separation are meaningless.

life is a circle

Keeping our dead with us, talking to them, including them in our lives, imagining heaven as a few inches above our heads or eternity as here and now – this is in no way to deny the reality of death. It is rather to see death differently from the conventional way in which modern society sees it, as an end, something to be dreaded.

We tend to look at life as though it were a straight line from birth to death. The longer the line, the more we imagine that we have lived. But life isn't like that. In the Native American culture, for example, life is seen not as linear, but rather as circular, and once the circle has been completed, at puberty, the person is whole, and the circle continues to expand outwards. In the Native American wisdom, wholeness is not seen as the duration one has lived, but the fullness with which one enters each complete moment.

The Celts also saw life as a circle. They had a sense of the rhythm of life. For them, the year had a rhythm of seasons, one moving into the other, and the day too had its rhythm with the dawn giving way to the noonday, the noonday to the evening, and the evening to darkness. The person also had a rhythm of growth and decline: *fiche blian ag fás, fiche blian faoi bhláth, fiche blian faoi neart, fiche blian ag dul ar ais* (twenty years a-growing, twenty years in flower, twenty years in strength, twenty years returning).

With the coming of Christianity to Ireland, the Celts adapted the new religious icons to suit their traditions. They superimposed a Celtic circle on the Christian cross, so that the pain of the cross was encircled by the symbol of life.

facing death

We live in an age that is obsessed with health, diet, how we look, whether we are getting enough of this or eating too much of that. We spend millions on cosmetics, on hair dyes, on trying to lose weight. We look on the change in our metabolism as we age, the lowering of our energy, the greying at the temples, the loss of hair as things to be denied and conquered rather than accepted as a normal part of living and as part of dying. The reason we are so obsessed with these things is that we are afraid of death.

We fear sickness too as we fear ageing and death. Nobody wants to be sick, nobody would choose it for themselves; and yet to learn to live with illness and suffering, even in small ways, is to learn to live and to learn to die. A friend of mine who was diagnosed as having cancer told me what hearing the news meant to her: 'At last I acknowledged that death was real. It did not mean that I would die immediately or even that I would die in six months; it simply meant that I would die at all.' For her, the diagnosis of her illness, although naturally a shock and an unpleasant piece of news, was an opportunity to face the idea of death.

Grief too is part of our daily existence, but we seldom recognise that pain that is very deep in all our hearts, a deep weeping, a mourning for things that are gone. Learning to live with grief, like learning to live with illness, is learning to live with our own vulnerability and our own mortality, and learning to acknowledge and accept death is learning to acknowledge impermanence. The acknowledgement of impermanence is the key to life itself. Facing death tunes us deeply into the life we imagine we will lose when we die. If we cannot believe that life and death are one, if we don't trust that sense of endlessness that is within us all, then our suffering is caused not so much by grief and pain and illness and fear but by holding on to our notions of how things might have been, could have been, should have been.

Life is about dying as well as about living. It is tragic if we are too busy denying death to be able to enjoy living. 'Some people are so afraid to die that they never begin to live,' says the American poet Henry Van Dyke.

Those who are most alive are those who want the truth more than life itself. If we want life more than truth, we seldom touch the truth of our life, but if truth is our priority, death will set us free and only the truth will continue. Death is a letting go of control. When we let go of control, only the truth remains and we can start responding from that moment.

Death is a necessary part of life. We all know that in our hearts. There has to be death in order for there to be new life. There is a time to die, to trust life and to surrender to death and to the process of time. It is only when we die that life can begin to grow again, that the circle can be renewed and sustained.

If we can live life with a sense of wholeness that includes death as part of life, we will find death less threatening and illness less fearful. Accepting the inevitability of death and the importance of death in the circle of life allows us to stay in the living present, to live a life that focuses on each precious moment, participating in life while realising that in doing so we are participating in dying too, because life and death are one and life is made up of a series of little dyings.

If we accept death as part of life, if we acknowledge that we are dying a little every day, then we will not postpone the showing of affection, the kind deed, the loving word; instead of leaving it until the person's last day when it is too late, when the appreciative word is unsaid and the good deed unaccomplished, we will do it now, because the time is now. If we express our positive feelings and attitudes, now, today and daily, then there will be no regrets when our friends have gone the silent way and we will not be left with nagging doubts about how things were between us.

letting go

Denying death is a fruitless and desperate holding on to things that ultimately we will have to relinquish in any case – health, youth, possessions – but accepting death is letting go whatever it is within us that fetters our souls. It takes patience and trust to learn to let go, but that letting go is living life to the full. In letting go we discover a new life, a new kind of living.

We all know people who are free because they can let go freely, readily and happily. I know a contemplative sister, aged 75, who was living in a hermitage on Achill Island off the west coast of Ireland. She felt called to live amongst the poor in the inner city of Dublin, and so she just let go of that life of peace, simplicity and rural isolation and came, with two small bags and a box, to live in a tiny bedsit in one of Focus Ireland's houses. The morning after she arrived, I asked her how she had slept, because I was aware that she was now in a much noisier place than she was used to. To my surprise, she replied that she had slept like a log. She had come to find a new life, and she had simply let go of the old one. She is now happily living her contemplative life amongst the city's poor.

Letting go is a kind of dying; it is like dying into freedom, like sinking into a new security on a different level. There is always something to let go; there is always another level that we can move to, another level of freedom and love. Often we are afraid to take the step, to let go of this or that, maybe a thing, a memory, an experience, a belief, a thought. We are afraid that when the process is over we will be lost, because we will have let go of what we knew. If we have left the place we knew, we may not be able to find our way back into that place again, and that is a frightening thought for us.

We all know people who are hangers on, people who still want to be in charge at the age of 65, 70, 75, people who no longer have the imagination or the energy for their positions and yet they hold on; even though life has changed around them in a way that they don't understand, they have not changed. These are people who cannot let go. They cannot give way to the new, to the creative in themselves, to the mystic in themselves that is waiting to be born.

In all our lives we meet situations where we have to let go, even if we don't want to. When somebody dies, when somebody betrays us, when somebody is unfaithful to us, it can be shattering, it can be embittering, it can poison us. But these situations give us choices. If we choose to let them go, we can be transformed. In this way, painful experiences can be fruitful and, despite the hurt, can be our opportunity to grow, if we can make that choice, if we can take that risk.

It is not easy to die to old ways, but letting go does more than break with some of our past and deplete what we thought was important. Every little death we die, every little letting go, turns us into something new. Every search, every new question about what is, forms and shapes us, and it brings new freedom, new life.

'don't know'

Letting go means living with the greyness and foggy insecurity of life. The Korean Zen master Seung Sahn teaches that we must learn to trust this land of 'don't know', because it is from here that wisdom comes forth. When we trust the 'don't know' we do not cling to the past, we do not hold on to old points of view and stagnant opinions. When we trust 'don't know', we are open to being a process with many different possibilities and alternatives, we do not force things to happen. 'Don't know' waits and explores, searches and considers, examines and trusts.

The long-timer practitioner and teacher of Buddhist meditation, Steven Levine, says, 'The difference between confusion and "don't know" is that confusion can only see one way and that way is blocked, while "don't know" is open to miracles and insights.' Living with 'don't know' is letting go. It means waiting, accepting the not knowing.

Having to wait is hard, especially for us, who live in an age where we expect and demand that things happen instantaneously. And yet if we are not prepared to wait, we can miss the transcendent when it happens. I have a large castor-oil plant in my room, and I watch it and wait for the leaves to unfold. They do this so slowly, it seems a terribly long process, and yet it does happen, the new leaves do unfurl, in their own time. The waiting time is providing time for growth. Nor Hall, the American feminist and poet, says, 'Letting things come of their own accord, or grow in their own time, often looks and feels like complete stagnation, but angels come out of those depths.'

Waiting is not passive; if we choose to wait in a lost space, with our insecurities and our uncertainties, knowing that the time is not yet right for us, it is in fact a very active thing. This waiting place, this land of nowhere, is actually the land of growth; when we feel that nothing is happening, that we are just roaming around inside ourselves, that is the time when something very important may be changing within us.

To live a detached life in the midst of attachment is not easy. To remain intimately connected with our own people, our community, our country, while distancing ourselves enough from them to be free and to be able to critique them is not easy. To renounce certain goods and advantages for the sake of more total possession of ourselves isn't easy. To surrender standards of success in order to share the life and the values of those who must struggle is not easy.

But if we let go, we will be able to live with ambiguity and with questions and we will know that these questions will, in their own time, become the answers. If we let go we will be able to understand and define in a new way what is permanent and secure, and it is only then that we can go freely from place to place without clinging to anything, to dreams, to possessions, to people, to status, even to life itself. When we let go, we are actually letting go to ourselves; what we give away is given to ourselves. We can only take with us when we die what we let go of when we were alive.

A TIME TO SOW

I was born and grew up in Dingle, in the county of Kerry, on the southwest coast of Ireland, a place of extraordinary natural beauty, where the people lived a life of great simplicity. When I was growing up in Kerry, everything had its time and everything had its season, and the lives of the people were governed by and interconnected with the life of the natural world and with the seasons. My people were farmers, people of the soil, and I suppose it is for this reason that I have always felt a great closeness to and kinship with the soil and with the land.

my father sowing

When I was growing up, one season of the year when special care had to be taken was the time for sowing the seed. The sowing didn't just happen; it had to be prepared for. I remember spending days with my father removing the stones from the fields, very early in the spring, gathering them together in little mounds. They were carried away later to be used for building dykes. As well as doing his preparatory work properly, the sower had to have great knowledge of the soil. Each field was different, each field was known by its own name, and the yield from each field was fairly predictable, if the farmer knew his business and went about his sowing and cultivating in the right way.

The memory I have of my father the farmer, my father the sower, is a memory of someone who was very centred on what he was doing. I often watched him looking at the land, looking at the soil, looking at a field over and over and over again as if he was meditating on it, before he ever sowed the field, and even as he sowed it, he stopped and looked and looked again before continuing with the sowing. He stopped and looked and reflected and watched. Rushing things was not part of his nature; nor is it part of the nature of sowing the seed. Contriving does not go hand in hand with sowing either, and he knew that. He knew that when things became too facile, too easy, too cute, it was time to push them away because they weren't in keeping with nature, with the earth and with the skill of the sower.

As a child I didn't know why he always stopped before he started anything, but looking back on it now, I realise that of course he was assessing the land, thinking about it, weighing up the possibilities, but I also think his stopping and looking at it was a sort of ritual or prayer, a blessing on the work he was about to undertake.

My life is not like that. I live an urban life and a frenetic one, far removed from the steady, reflective life of the farm. I am one of those people who is always busy, always rushing around, making phone calls, taking phone calls, going to meetings, making things happen, writing things in my diary, crossing things out of my diary, talking to people, making plans, making appointments, keeping appointments, thinking up schemes, driving to Cork or Limerick or Waterford and driving home again the same day, giving talks, catching planes to far-off places like Venezuela or Nigeria or San Francisco, getting my passport renewed, getting visas sorted out, remembering to get vaccinations, forgetting to get vaccinations, visiting my family, visiting sick and dying people, the homeless people who have for many years been the centre of my work, going to weddings and funerals, celebrations and parties, writing newspaper articles, writing books.

I love my way of life, but I fear it too, because I know how easily all the traffic and the movement and the coming and going can prevent me from taking root, from settling down and taking time to do the really important things like being still and calm and keeping in touch with my inner being.

taking time to reflect

I often think of my father as I start work each day or when I start into anything new, a meeting, an exchange, an interview or a phone call. Sometimes I can go into my office, and before I know it I have my pen or the phone in my hand and I am lost in what I do.

This is not the way my father went about his work of sowing the seed, beginning by being still, standing erect in his field in respect for the soil. When I think about him doing that, it reminds me to make the time and take the trouble to stop for reflection or a little prayer before starting on a job or an enterprise or making a phone call. In fact, we have a practice in the Sisters of Charity that we stop and pray before we do each task in the day, but I sometimes forget, and it is the thought of my father that reminds me.

If I don't make the conscious effort to do this, I find myself skating on the surface of what I am doing, I feel ungrounded and I become easily agitated when things don't go smoothly. I know that I need to take the time to centre my breathing, to pray or perform a ritual that is meaningful to me. That makes me present to myself and to the task before me and brings a new balance as I start into any situation, reconnecting me with the deep creative, divine currents within and around me.

process, not product

To sow is to be centred, focused, grounded. The sower surrenders to the earth and to the creator. Behaving like the sower in our approach to our work, grounding ourselves before we start, preparing for the task, taking time to stop and reflect, is surrendering to the process of the work, letting go of the idea of the end product. Working with the finished product always in mind is paralysing for the sower, preventing and crippling the process of surrendering to the earth, which is what sowing is about.

Similarly, focusing too much on the product can be counterproductive for anyone in their work. If we don't surrender to the processes of our work, what we do will be contrived and manipulated. It may ostensibly be successful, but it will not be truly fruitful.

interconnections

All things on earth are interconnected. It is the sowers of this world who know that most surely. John Muir, the great naturalist and ecologist, said, 'When we try to pick out anything by itself, we find it hitched to everything else in the universe.' Sowing, surrendering to the processes of the earth or of work and of life, puts us in touch with that deep interconnectedness of things. We are interconnected not only with each other, but with the trees and the whales and the wolves and the flowers and with all living things that share the same space we do.

We are interconnected not only here and now, in this time and in this space, but with everything in the past and in the future and into that unknown dimension we call eternity. Oscar Wilde said, 'We think in eternity, but we move slowly through time.' Shakespeare put it like this:

> Like as the waves make towards the pebbled shore
> So do our minutes hasten to their end;
> Each changing place with that which goes before
> In sequent toil, all forwards do contend.

(SONNET 60)

If we have a sense of interconnectedness across time and into eternity, then just as we know that the personal self will sail only in the river of this lifetime, we know that the universal self will sail far greater oceans. There is an eternal region within us. The great medieval English mystic, Julian of Norwich, described it in these words: 'God never began to love us. God has loved us for all eternity. We were all born into each other.'

For the painter Vincent van Gogh, whose bright and powerful work we all know so well from posters and postcards even if we haven't had the chance to see it in reality, the soil was a symbol of a 'longing for the infinite'. This longing for the infinite resides in every human heart. It is an indication of the sense of the divine that is at the core of our being. That point of divinity at the centre of our being flows into the divine energy that embraces us, and we return home as a drop of water returns as rain to the sea from which it was born.

Van Gogh had a sense of the interconnectedness of the painter and what he painted:

> If we study Japanese art, we see an artist who is wise, philosophical and intelligent in how he spends his time. He studies a single blade of grass, this blade of grass leads him to draw the plant and then the season, the wide aspects of the countryside, the animals, then the human figures. So he passes his life. Isn't it almost an act of religion which these simple Japanese teach us who live in nature as though they themselves were flowers? We must return to nature in spite of our education and our work in a world of convention. You cannot study Japanese art without becoming happier.

Acknowledging the interconnectedness of all things is an act of spiritual intimacy, a most profound interaction with the world. Being aware that we are in communion with all people, all creatures and all things liberates us from the imprisonment of alienation. If we see ourselves as separate creatures, then we fight for survival, we devour everything in sight, we destroy trees, water, animals, the air, even space, without concern or awareness of the effects we are having on our environment and on the earth. But if we experience the interconnectedness of all things, then suddenly we are awakened to the sacred vitality of the earth and its life forms. This is a truly transforming experience.

cherishing the weeds

When I was a child growing up in rural Ireland, we were encouraged to pull the weeds so that the crops could grow. But instead of throwing away the weeds, we were made to bury them in the soil, because they could provide nourishment for the growing plants. At the time, I thought this practice had to do with not being wasteful; I see now that there was more to it than just being frugal. Using the weeds in this way was an expression of the belief that everything in nature had its place; nothing was useless; everything is part of life.

Years later I was surprised and interested to read that cherishing the weeds is a valued Zen practice. The great Japanese Zen master, Suzuki Shunryu (who founded the Zen Mountain Centre in California, the first Zen monastery outside Asia) repeatedly exhorted his followers to 'mind weeds':

> *Mind weeds. You should rather be grateful for the weeds you have in your mind because eventually they will enrich your practice... they change into self-nourishment.*

sowers hope

The sower sows the seed, in the sure and certain expectation that the seed will germinate and the plant will grow. The sower is a person of hope.

Hope is not just one single quality or promise. Hope has to do with believing beyond knowing that there is a garden of beauty that awaits us. Hope encourages us to follow our dreams, to believe in the part of us that envisions a new way. Hope is trusting that what is happening will eventually make sense and that even if it never does become meaningful it will still offer an opportunity for growth. Hope assures us each morning that our life is of value, no matter how unsettling or disturbing it may be. Hope encourages our hearts not to give up and urges us when it is time to move on. Hope doesn't need words or proofs or conditions. Hope accepts mystery and offers the gift of solid trust to the unknown. Hope doesn't pretend it is going to be easy. Wherever there is hope, there is also struggle. Sometimes the hope may be fragile, it may be hard to reach but it is always there for the sowers:

> *Hope is a thing with feathers*
> *that perches in the soul*
> *and sings the tune without the words*
> *and never stops at all.*

EMILY DICKINSON

Sowing is not easy. It is hard work. It involves going out in the early days of the year, often before the weather has become mild, and toiling over the soil, trusting that it will, over time, yield up its harvest. The sower is willing to accept that life will always be made of hills and valleys, of light and darkness, and that we live always with creative tension, in the world and within ourselves.

The poet and spiritual writer May Sarton says,

> *It is only when we can believe that we are creating the soul that life has any meaning, but when we can believe it, and I do and always have, then there is nothing to do that is without meaning and nothing at all that exists that does not hold the seed of creation in it.*

That is the hope of the sower. That is the hope in the child who discovers the secret garden, the much-neglected place of beauty. Hope is what the children in the story *The Secret Garden* had as they weeded and cleaned the neglected garden and excitedly planted flower seeds in it and waited and believed the flowers would take root and grow – and they did.

sowers are life-givers

Artists are sowers. As one of my favourite poets, the early twentieth-century German lyric poet, Rainer Maria Rilke wrote:

> *Everything is gestation and then birthing. To let each impression and each embryo of a feeling come to completion entirely in itself in the dark in the unsayable, the unconscious, beyond the reach of one's own understanding and with deep humility and patience, to wait for the hour when a new clarity is born, this alone is what it means to be an artist in understanding as well as in creating.*

The famous artist Marc Chagall once said: 'In art as in life everything is possible as long as it is based on love.' Sowing is an affirmation that everything is possible as long as it is based on love. This may seem a romantic view of life, but the evidence surrounds us. The sower feels the breeze caressing her skin, listens to the leaves rustling in the wind, looks at the morning dew adorning the spider's web and watches the night give way to day and season give way to season. She loves the seeds in the earth into life as a baby is loved into life. Every baby is born out of the darkness of the womb, every plant from the dark of the earth. The sower says Yes to life, Yes, Yes, Yes. Yes is the expression of the sower.

The sower accepts the sacredness of life and sees the generative energy in the soil, in the rain, in the sun, in the day and in the night. The sower is open to the generative energy and love within her and around her. The sower knows the secret of growth, the slow process that needs its own time. The sower knows what it is like, waiting for life to emerge. Sowing is about releasing life, about releasing hidden beauty and potential, often silently, as the figures in Michelangelo's wonderful and moving half-finished sculpture, *Prisoners in Stone,* are captured forever at the point where they are emerging from the stone, partly free and alive, but partly imprisoned, lodged in the lump of stone, waiting to be released.

patience and surprise

The season of springtime is when the sower comes into his or her own. The hope that a sower has is a hope that comes from letting the past be, from turning it under like the turning under of the spring soil when a new crop is planted. The sower connects himself or herself with the soil. This gives the sower an inner freedom and makes his or her body, mind and spirit one with the whole of creation.

The sower marvels to see the power of life pushing up the buds from the earth. That marvel repeats itself, spring, after spring, after spring. Even though that is exactly what the sower expected to happen, it is always a surprise to see the soil responding to the sun above and the moisture below, to see the first blades of green pushing up through the soil, the plant strengthening and growing, the crop thickening on the stem or the fruit swelling on the branches.

These marvels and surprises are bound to happen, yet they can't be rushed. It all happens in its own time. No baby has a sign on it that says what moment it is going to be born. The baby and the mother must wait until the push of the contractions will toss the door of the womb open. No seed in the soil has a sign that says it is to shoot up this way or on that day. It will have to wait until the warmth of the soil penetrates the earth and draws forth the green of the flower. No butterfly in its chrysalis has a timekeeper. She waits and waits and has to hand herself over to the unfolding process of life through creation.

Life unfolds everywhere at its own rate. There is no way of knowing how the seed we have planted is doing. We can't dig it up each day and check it out. To do that would be to bring death. We have to be patient, to be hopeful, and to trust. That is the great lesson of sowing, learning to wait, learning to let life take its course. There may be plenty of inner stirrings, but we must trust what we cannot see. The sower must trust the process, wait, believe, be patient and hope, and in the end, the sower is rewarded with surprise.

sowing for the future

We can all be sowers of our time, people who sow the seeds that will be reaped by the next generation. When we sow, we must not expect instant success, but sow we must if a new world is ever to come to fruit. The purpose of our generation is to sow the seeds that will make a better world possible in the future and to prepare for it.

Making a new and better life for the next generation means anticipating and creating change, but not change as we have come to think of it. To live is to change, to live fully is to change often, we are told. In an age driven by information technology and global communication, change is happening at a faster pace than we could have imagined even ten years ago. We live in a culture that takes rapid change for granted, and the more rapid it is the better it seems. But the life of the spirit is not about change of that sort; it is about living in a way that will be fruitful for ourselves and about creating the conditions where our children and our children's children can live fruitful lives.

Real change, the kind of change that affects the mind and heart and that truly makes the world a better place, is not instant; it is slow, it is like the seed coming to life in the earth, it is laborious, it is painful, it does not come easily to many of us. It costs us something and it demands a price. The price it demands is a change of heart.

Even in the face of the impossible, we must act as if it is possible to change the world, to make it a better place for the next generation. That is what hope is. That is what sowing is about. It is living with uncertainty and ambiguity. It is living with hope and hoping against hope.

sowers have vision

Sowing is virtually impossible for those of us who are simply seeking success. It is taking hundreds of thousands of years to eliminate slavery, poverty, racism and sexism. We all talk about it and yet we allow it to go on around us before our very eyes. Most of us haven't got the sower's courage, the courage to go on and on planting new questions in the human heart and soul.

Sowing isn't easy. It takes a long, long time, and we must be prepared never to see the result of our work. The results may have to be left to a generation of harvesters in the future. The American poet and songwriter Ruben Alves wrote: 'Let us plant dates even though those who plant them will never eat them... We must live by the love of what we will never see...'

For now there is only the long, tiresome chore of planting small seeds in dark ground, and waiting to see what, if anything, grows. The process of sowing may be a long and empty one, which requires infinite patience. It is looking for something that others don't even know is lacking. People listen but do not believe, or they listen but do not hear. Some people cannot hear because they cannot see issues or problems, or what is lacking, unless they see the solutions. Some people do not hear because they are too satisfied with the way things are.

The business of sowing is like prophesying. Prophesying is about changing people's hearts, changing the way people think. This requires the courage to go alone on an unknown path, to make the path by walking it. It is not for those who seek immediate success; it is for people who live according to what is in their heart, according to what their heart is telling them about what life is meant to be like. It may mean being ridiculed, being called naive, soft or wet.

Sowing is about believing that there is a time for everything. It is our task to carry out our work without ceasing, never knowing where the seed will take root, never quitting. It is a slow and arduous task, involving a process of waiting and waiting in hope, with conviction and with expectation, in an age of immediacy and instant results.

The sower, like the prophet, is not concerned with success. His or her life is lived at the edge, planting the questions and possibilities in human hearts, never knowing what effect they will have, never seeking results and being prepared to live with the questions.'

To sow is to live with trust and conviction that goes beyond the ordinary and it is wanting something badly enough in the future to give all of life preparing for it now, often alone, often unnoticed or even rejected and often not seeing the result. It is about living with trust, abandonment, vision and conviction.

Prophets often don't see the results of what they have worked for. They didn't see the end of slavery, they didn't see the end of poverty, they didn't see the end of racism and sexism. What they see is a vision. In their efforts to realise the vision, they may fail and fail and fail again – but they try and try and try again, and in their trying they are beacon lights of hope for many.

The prophet or sower must live with human weakness and frailty. The prophet knows harsh reality. Prophets are people with their feet on the ground, but with their minds and hearts filled with fiery dreams. They touch the sky and walk the earth. The sower's or prophet's dream is God's dream for our time. That time is now – always now, whatever the future, however long it takes.

A TIME TO REAP

*Sow integrity for yourselves, reap a harvest of kindness; break up your
fallow ground, it is time to go seeking Yahweh.*

HOSEA, 10:12

Reaping time or harvest time was one of the times of the year that I
enjoyed most as a child. People came together for the harvesting of
the crops and for the threshing of the corn, and there was a festive
feeling in the air. At harvest time, the people forgot all the hard work
of sowing and cultivation; they forgot about the crops that had failed;
they forgot all the things that had gone wrong during the farming
year. They set all those mishaps and stresses aside at this time and
they celebrated the crops that had matured and ripened and were
now being harvested.

accepting ourselves

Harvest is a time to celebrate what we have and to rejoice in the
present. It is a time of strength, a time of hope, a time of confidence,
and a time for celebrating and accepting what is, not for thinking of

what is past or what might have been or for fantasising about the future. The harvest is now.

It is not always easy for us to accept what is, or to accept ourselves as we are. If we want to be reapers, to be able to celebrate the harvest of ourselves, the first choice we need to make is to accept ourselves as we are, with our gifts and our abilities and also with our short-comings, our inner wounds, our darkness and our mortality. I was talking recently to a woman who told me that she has not worn a skirt for years. She was raped as a young woman, and it is only now, years later, that she is gradually learning to accept her womanhood. Most of us haven't had such a horrific experience, but we all have our inner wounds and because of those wounds, those feelings of inadequacy or guilt or whatever it may be, we may find ourselves running away from ourselves, denying our true selves. To cover up our feelings of inadequacy or despair, we want to be more important, we want to be more glamorous, we want to be richer, we want to be better, we want to be more successful. We want to be somebody else. But if we spend our lives trying to be somebody else, we will live lives of frustration and we will never be able to reap the fruits that are intended for us.

We can only begin the process of reaping if we are prepared to give up dreaming about a different self, a dream self, an idealised self, an unreal self. Through the process of accepting ourselves and who we are, we regain the inner energy that is otherwise focused on hiding our wounds – our faults, our failings, our struggles. It is by facing our wounds and our struggles that we discover what it is that gives our lives direction and meaning, and that is what it is to reap.

age and wisdom

A few years ago now, I spent some time in Berkeley in California. While I was there, one of the lecturers at the university held a party. She was sixty, and she wanted to celebrate it and announce that she was now a 'crone'. She had gained a lot from life and now she wanted to gather it up and celebrate it. She was now a wise woman, a woman of grace and wisdom, a woman who was slowing down and going deeper into her self, into her soul, in order to reap the harvest of her life. She was ready now to share that harvest with others, to become a resource for other people. Rather than being afraid for her future, as people approaching old age sometimes are, she was accepting herself and her age and celebrating it. She was doing what the great Christian writer Thomas Merton described as finding 'this true interior self, which must be drawn up like a jewel from the bottom of the sea'.

I was intrigued by this idea of celebrating the onset of old age, the age of wisdom, the harvest age or the time of reaping. When I was growing up, people didn't announce themselves in that Californian sort of way, of course, but there were elderly men and women who emerged as people of wisdom in the community, who were looked up to and whose advice was sought and freely given. One wise woman I remember particularly was the midwife on the peninsula. She knew every child and their parents, and as she grew older she radiated a graciousness and contentment and a deep wisdom to all of us. The very presence of people like her gave assurance and confidence to the people and to the neighbourhood.

All old communities and cultures have their people of wisdom, their elders, who are looked up to and respected, but modern urban people in general don't have that resource of wisdom in their midst. That's partly because people who live in towns and cities tend not to know each other very well; they have lost their sense of community. But it's also because we no longer acknowledge the beauty of ageing and the wisdom of the aged.

In our society, growing old is seen as a process to be feared. We think of older people as people who lack joy in their lives, who lack purpose, who lack understanding and who lack value. This makes it all the more difficult for us to face the reality of change as we grow older. We see change happening in us, every part of us, our bodies, our energy, our strength, our sleep patterns, our ability to remember, all are changing. As we see our parents and friends begin to die, we are faced with our own mortality, and that can be difficult. Of course we need not become prematurely old or 'die' before our time by anticipating death, but at the same time, there is no point in trying to hold on desperately to our youth, obstinately denying our ageing. Instead, if we can enjoy what we have learned and what we have become, we then have something to pass on, a legacy to leave to the next generation. Old age, the harvest time of life, can be a time to gather up all the experience of our lives, to celebrate it, and to share it with our friends and neighbours. As we grow older, we can all become crones, we can all become mentors, people of grace and wisdom that younger people love to have around. Being honest about our own struggles and our fears and hopes is the best gift we can pass on to others.

Old age is a particular time of reaping, but reaping needn't be confined to the end of our lives. We can reap also at the end of every day and every year. The time to reap, to appreciate, enjoy and celebrate our gifts, is now, every day and all these 'nows' flow into the final harvesting at the close of life.

sitting still

Harvest is a time for reaping the gifts that we have been blessed with, gifts that have been awakened, developed and affirmed. Deep within each of us there is a knowing place. When we spend time there, tending the gifts that we have been given, we discover how fruitful our life has been and how much we can share with the world. Each person has his or her secret or mystery, his or her particular journey, his or her vocation to grow. But if we don't spend time being still, being with ourselves in that knowing place, we may never realise our fruitfulness, never reap our harvest.

In Willa Cather's novel, *O Pioneers*, the character Alexandria takes charge of the family farm of wild and difficult land after her father's death. A former neighbour returns from his new life in the city many years later and is amazed at what Alexandria has done with the land. At one point in the story she says to him: 'We hadn't, any of us, much to do with it. The land did it. It had its little joke. It pretended to be poor because nobody knew how to work it right and then all at once it worked itself, it woke up out of its sleep and stretched itself and it was so big, so rich and we suddenly found we were rich, just from sitting still.' The land of our heart is like that. It too has its little jokes. We think it is poor soil because we don't know how to work it, but when we learn to do our inner work, to be patient and wait and tenderly watch, it will wake up and work itself and we will be rich just from sitting still.

It's not easy, though, for us to learn to sit still and tend the land of our heart. We are taught that we are what we achieve, that more is better, that everything has to be earned – money, career, recognition, affirmation, even affection. What we achieve is what makes us happy and we value ourselves and others according to what we and they have achieved. This obsession with achievement makes it difficult to learn to be still with ourselves and to accept who we are, as we are.

Reaping is the opposite of being obsessed with achievement and success. The reaper in us lives and works out of love with no assurance of success. Considering achievement more important than trying is not reaping; considering answers more important than questions is not reaping.

Reaping has more to do with being than with doing, with being fruitful than with achieving success. Being fruitful means fulfilling each day and becoming each day more and more what we are called to be. Being fruitful is being true to ourselves, in the knowledge that there is a higher power than ourselves.

The reaper within us moves us from challenge to challenge in life with a trusting soul, from season to season with hope and joy, always ready to plant again. The reaper's sense of purpose enlivens each generation, raises questions, resisting easy answers, refusing false success.

fruitfulness

People often wait for the perfect time to do a thing, but there is no really perfect time for anything. We wait for the perfect time to make that difficult decision, we wait for the perfect time to make the change that we know is inescapable, and the harvesting of which we could have been a part is put off in the hope of another day. There is always a right time to reap, and that time is always now. What we do not reap now we miss, and once missed, we can never reclaim it.

The great American naturalist and thinker Thoreau said: 'We must walk consciously only part way towards our goal, and then leap in the dark to our success.' The success Thoreau speaks about here is what I am calling 'fruitfulness'. This sort of success, this fruitfulness, depends on a leap in the dark, on taking the chance that this moment is the right moment, the right moment for us to do what we must, and that is all.

A TIME TO REVERENCE
THE EARTH

Ask the cattle, seek information from the birds of the air; the creeping things of the earth will give you lessons and the fishes of the sea will tell you all.

JOB 12: 7-8

As a society, as a people, we modern westerners are destroying the earth. And yet, if we have the capacity to destroy it, we can surely save it too, if we so choose. Now is the time for us to reach out and embrace the earth anew, to play with the wind, to seek beauty in life's becoming.

The earth is revealing itself to us today as it never has before, and in today's polluted and damaged world we need to be more alert than ever to what the earth is telling us. Now more than ever, with the earth in such danger, we need to be aware that we are intimately connected to our environment, to realise that we are in the earth, and the earth is in us.

loving the earth
If we are to hear what the earth is telling us and demanding of us, we need to give up old ways of seeing the earth and relating to her. We

need to realise that our needs will be met only if we respond to the earth's cry for help. To do that we need a new kind of love for the earth.

Our love has been too anthropocentric, seeing the earth as belonging to us rather than us as belonging to the earth. Our approach to loving the earth has been partial: we have had an unbalanced concern for parts of the earth, our own private gardens, rather than the whole earth. Of course we love our gardens, and that is right and good, but we need to extend our love beyond our own little hedged-in patches.

To love the earth more, and to love the whole earth, we must learn to love ourselves less. This is not easy for people like us, who live in an age where the messages we are bombarded with are about how to be loved rather than about how to be loving.

new rituals

To learn to love the earth more, we need, first, new parables and new rituals to remind us of the beauty of the earth and the life it supports. In the Hindu parable of Indra's net, the god Indra casts his net of life into the voids of space. At each intersection of threads in the net, there is a crystal bead. Each bead is a living thing, shining radiantly into space, and each crystal bead in the net of life reflects the glow of every other bead. According to the parable, this is how life works on earth: each living thing is a spark of sunlit energy, a crystal bead in the net of life, glowing with its own radiance and also reflecting the other beads.

The Native Americans have a prayer for when they walk on the grass: 'Let me so walk upon you that even though you must bend your head under me as I pass by, you will know after I have gone that I am your sister.' In India, children are taught by their mothers to pat the earth each morning on waking up, to apologise for walking on it. We too need reminders like this to focus our attention on what is truly important. We need, like Kavanagh, to be able to find a 'star-lovely art/In a dark sod.'

enjoying the earth

Secondly, we need to stop and look and enjoy, to appreciate and revere the earth. In order to do this, we need to realise that, like all forms of life, we are only here for a few moments.

A story is told about an old lady called Ashley Montagu who was asked how she remained so youthful at the age of 72; she replied, 'The trick is to die young as late as possible.' Instead of striving to die young as late as possible, or to remain as young and as childlike as we can for as long as we can, we often get caught up in our projects, thinking, judging, doing, so that if we are not careful we can grow old without even noticing, without being, without ever getting in touch with the earth.

The story of the origins of Zen tells how the founder of Buddhism had been asked to present a talk on truth to his followers. However, instead of talking, he merely took a flower from a nearby vase and gazed at it. Everyone was puzzled by this behaviour, but suddenly one person smiled knowingly. In a sudden flash he recognised the point the Buddha was making: words are just that, words and nothing more; reality lies in being, not in thinking or speaking. This disciple became the first teacher of Zen.

It is easy to become so full of our own importance, to get so caught up with our role-playing and posturing and verbalising about things that we miss who and what we really are. The American philosopher Alan Watts suggests that much of what we do is merely attention-seeking antics and that we fail miserably to notice what is really happening, the heart of the matter:

> ... perhaps the reason for [our] love of non-human nature is that communion with it restores to us a level of our own human nature at which we are still sane, free from humbug, and untouched by anxieties about the meaning and purpose of our lives. For what we call 'nature' is free from a certain kind of scheming and self-importance.

To get out of our own light, out of our own way, we must take unusual steps. This could perhaps be something as simple as going out at night without a light. Wendell Berry says:

> *To go in the dark with a light is to know the light. To know the dark, go dark. Go without sight, and find that the dark, too, blooms and sings, and is travelled by dark feet and dark wings.*

keeping watch

The world in which we live and work is very complex and very fragile. Throughout history we have had good reason to fear for the very future of the earth. The focus of our fear in the recent past was nuclear weapons; now we need also to be capable of recognising the signs of impending ecological disaster.

The third thing we need in order to learn to love the earth anew is to be watchful, to call attention to the dangers ahead, just as on ships men stood watch through the night, prepared to alert the passengers to the unseen dangers. As we sail through life on the earth, the dangers are all here on board with us, and we need a new generation to sound an alarm, a new crew of men and women to help to set us on a safe course. There is no doubt but that there is trouble and turbulence ahead. What we need is to be alert to it.

complacency

At one level we already know about the trouble there is ahead and about the trouble that is brewing here on the earth – toxic waste, the reckless use and thoughtless abuse of animals, global warming and the depletion of the ozone layer – but we tend to set thoughts of these things aside, to put them out of our minds. This is partly, no doubt, because we haven't, until very recently, had the basic scientific information and because scientists themselves have not been in agreement about the causes of ecological problems, but it is also because powerful business interests tend to hide or minimise the obvious, blatant harm their businesses are doing to the earth.

Another reason we have been so complacent is that we are not confronted directly and immediately with the consequences of our abuse of the planet. The price to be paid for sustaining our lifestyle has not yet had to be paid by us; it is being paid by people in faraway places, and it will continue to be paid by generations to come, but so far, we ourselves have had to bear very few of the costs incurred by how we live our lives.

Nor have we really any comprehension of what the consequences would be in terms of energy consumption, the depletion of natural resources and the generation of waste and pollution if the developing world were to attain the standard of living that we already enjoy. Otherwise, we would not so naively wish that they could catch up with us and live as we do. In place of that wish, we need instead to imagine new ways for all of us to share the resources of the planet more equally – which would involve us in the West making do with less, rather than the poorer countries aspiring to more – and to look after them more carefully.

There is another reason too that we do not pay attention to the voices of those who warn us of what is happening and what will happen. It is because we do not pay attention to nature. We do not revere it. We treat it as an object. We can delight in its beauty, but for the most part it serves simply as the stage for our exploits and as a source of raw materials for our designs. Beckett's play *Endgame* is a powerful expression of the absurdity of the universe we create with our pretence of progressing towards an ever-improving human situation, which instead of bringing about a wonderworld is bringing about a waste world.

now is the time

Now is the time for all of us to face the challenge to understand, empower and support the work of those men and women who work for ecologically sound policies and practices. Now is the time to revere the earth as our mother and the sky as our father. For the earth is not *like* our mother – it *is* our first mother; the sky is not *like* our

51

father – it *is* our first father. Now is the time to examine our attitudes towards domination, acquisition and unnecessary consumption.

Now is the time to bring back into consciousness what we should never have forgotten: the earth does not belong to us; rather, we belong to the earth. We are part of the earth and she is part of us. We should remember this every time we touch the earth, every time we walk on it, every time we pray.

Our challenge is to view the earth not as humanity's warehouse or playground but as God's creation. Our challenge is to question the individualism, utilitarianism and greed that plague the modern attitude towards nature, especially in the Western world. Our challenge is to shape and influence the future.

new visions

This is a time when we need new visions for the earth. We need to have visions, dreams and symbols that are grand and powerful enough to change the world. We need the kind of creative imagination that Mozart had when he wrote *The Magic Flute,* or Dante when he wrote *The Divine Comedy;* the kind of imagination that gave Shakespeare the sensitivity and understanding that found expression in his plays.

We all have the capacity for vision. Very few of us are geniuses of the order of Mozart or Shakespeare, but we all share the visionary power that came to such glorious apotheosis in those acknowledged geniuses. We experience this visionary power most profoundly when we are immersed in the depth of our own being and in tune with the universe. Some visions unfold in our sleep, some in visionary waking moments. If we can seize these moments of vision, we can dream new dreams together.

Paraphrasing George Bernard Shaw, Robert Kennedy once said: 'Some men see things as they are, and say why; I dream things that never were and say why not.' Why not a world where the threat of nuclear annihilation is only a vague and unpleasant memory? Why not a world where the threat of ecological disaster is out of the question? Why not a world of small towns, spaced miles apart? Why not a world where all of us, not just some of us, pursue a physical labour-intensive lifestyle that is close to the earth? Why not a world where there are more tigers in the wild than in zoos? Why not a world where we can take down our anthropocentric structures and systems and put in place ecocentric structures and systems? Why not a world where we can find new stars to follow and new songs to sing? Why not a world where we can, as Thoreau suggests, build some foundations under our dreams?

listening to the earth

Above all, why not listen to the earth? The earth speaks only to those who can hear with their hearts. It speaks in a thousand small ways, but it sends messages without words. The earth speaks in the language of love. Its voice is in the shape a new leaf, the feel of a water-worn stone, the colour of the evening sky, the smell of summer rain, the sound of the night wind. The earth's whispers are everywhere, but only those who have slept and dreamt with it can respond to its call. The earth speaks in magic, the magic of rainbows and waterfalls and frogs, in the magic of interacting sunlight and air and water, and soil, creating a constantly shifting, rich kaleidoscope.

For the ancient peoples of the earth and for the peoples who still preserve, in some measure, those ancient cultures – the Aborigines, the Maoris, the Native Americans – the features of the earth are an everyday part of their living heritage. They read their life-story in the landscape itself. Every mountain, every river, every valley, speaks of ancient events. The Celtic people too had this sort of reverence for the earth. Their spirituality was truly earth- and creation-centred. Even in my own childhood, I experienced a life that was rooted in nature: everything had its place and every moment was related to the earth. It was magical.

Most of us living today's urban lifestyle have lost that connectedness with the earth, but one group of people are privileged to have it still in a most particular way. I don't mean farmers or gardeners or fisherfolk – though they too are specially gifted with a life that brings them close to the earth – but geologists. For geologists, as for 'primitive' peoples, the earth's features speak of ancient events, although of course in a very different way. For geologists, a hill or a valley is a glacial remnant, a canyon represents a timetable.

intimacy with the earth

For the earth-lover too, each fold, each depression, each peak in the crust of the planet speaks of new discoveries in a lifelong quest to seek out magical places, to be intimate with the earth and its life. For the earth-lover, the earth is a great adventure, an exciting experience that remains endlessly repeatable throughout life. This is no fleeting romance; it is an affair that is unconstrained by age or custom and strengthened rather than diminished by sharing. In fact, the more one gives it away, the stronger it grows and the more it returns to us.

For someone visiting the earth for the first time, the real treasures here would all be free: the smell of a sunlit meadow, the taste of a cold cup of spring water, the crunch of the snow under foot. These are just some of the supreme treasures of this magical garden in space, this precious oasis we call earth. Any space travellers who happened by would surely see earth as a stopping point for sustenance beyond the necessities of food and water; but if people from outer space really did visit us, would they not consider us earthlings a rather childish people who are unable control our appetites?

getting to know the earth

We can't all be environmental activists, dedicating our lives to saving the earth from ourselves, but one thing we can all do is to set aside some time, once a week perhaps, to get to know our place and our space. People of diverse religious backgrounds have in common a tradition of Sabbath, a day set aside for rest and prayer. More informally, many people also have a tradition of Sunday as a day for the out-of-doors. This is not at all a bad idea. Perhaps more of us could think about setting aside part of our Sabbath as a time for exploration and discovery and reverencing the earth. For we need a time that is dedicated to getting outside our structures, to leaving our little urban boxes, to spending time outdoors, celebrating the wonders of the earth, just one day a week enjoying our space and our place.

But we don't need to wait till Sunday to reverence the earth. Every day we could lift a fistful of earth and give thanks for the life it sustains; we could bend down and touch the grass; we could even greet the first tree that we meet each morning; we could listen, at least, to the rain.

St Francis

There is a story about St Francis, the great nature saint, enjoying the night air in his home village of Assisi. When the moon came up it was huge and luminous, lighting the entire earth with its radiance. Francis noticed that no one else was outside to enjoy the miracle, so he ran to the bell tower and began ringing the bell enthusiastically. When the people rushed from their houses in alarm and saw Francis at the top of the tower they called out, asking him what was wrong. Francis replied simply, 'Lift up your eyes, my friends, look at the moon.'

Sometimes all we need to hear the earth's voice is to get out of our heads, to get out of our little boxes, as the people of Assisi did on that evening. Often this means retreating from the world for a while, casting off the layers of synthetic and artificial substances with which we have encased ourselves. We all desperately need at times to put aside our human acquaintances for a while and get away from the world of words so that we can communicate on a different level with the earth. We have listened for too long to the voices of our own kind, forgetting that we share this earth also with multitudes of other forms of life. Since they do not speak our language we must seek them out and learn theirs.

Although the earth speaks to everyone, only a few respond. Some people can no longer hear the earth's song, because they have lost the ability to detect its harmony. Often we behave like bored teenagers who are being taken around, let's say, different parts of the west coast of Ireland and all that they can say is, 'Oh it's all the same, I've seen this view before.' If we want to retrieve our ability to appreciate and enjoy the earth, we need teachers who can help us to rebuild our sense of relationship with the earth, teachers who can remind us, as the poet Kahlil Gibran says, 'that the earth likes to feel your bare feet and the wind longs to play with your hair'.

our little pieces of earth

More of us in the West live now in cities, where the earth is barely visible, than on the land. We have our precious corners and patches of earth in cities too, of course, and we cherish them, our back gardens, our patio tubs, our hanging baskets, our window boxes. I live in inner-city Dublin and where I live we are developing a little organic 'sanctuary' or meditation garden. At first we thought it was not possible to do this in the middle of the city, but then we realised that, as the Native–American Black Elk, puts it: 'Anywhere is the center of the world.'

We can all make anywhere into the centre of our world, but we do need to keep in mind that even the centre of the world is not the whole world, and our little garden or our little patch of earth is just that – a little piece of something that is infinitely bigger and greater and grander than the little corner of it that we have made our own, something that is worth caring for and reverencing and passing on intact to our children.

A TIME FOR SOLITUDE

I am a person who lives a very full and hectic life. Often I wish it were not so hectic. People who know me and know how I am always flying around from one thing to another laugh when I tell them that my ambition is to be a contemplative, to withdraw from the bustle of the world and spend my time in prayer and meditation. Maybe they are right to laugh. Maybe I would miss my busy lifestyle more than I think I would, but what I do know for sure is that it is in the time I spend in solitude and quiet that I discover who I am and what my life's journey is all about. It is in solitude that I find I can forget about the things that bother me, that I can learn to see those things as essentially small things, and that I can allow myself to be opened up to wonder.

silence

In his lovely poem where he writes in the first person as silence, Brendan Kennelly says, 'Once I was the heartbeat of the world/But am an outcast now.' Silence is indeed a stranger to people who live in today's busy and noisy world. When I look back on the lives my parents and neighbours lived, I can see that they lived and worked for long stretches in silence and often also in solitude. My father worked in the fields, on the hillside and in the boglands, making and saving hay, cutting and saving turf, sowing and reaping corn, walking with sheep and cattle, horses and ponies, often in complete silence and solitude. Others worked out at sea, fishing in the light and in the dark, totally engrossed in the task at hand, sometimes with mates but also often in a solitude and silence that can only be appreciated by the experienced. Women like my mother worked in their kitchens, preparing food, making bread, churning butter, tending to and caring for flocks of chickens and ducks and milking the cows, feeding the calves. Many of these activities were carried out in silence and solitude, which gave the people an opportunity to lose themselves in thought, as they worked in tune with the things around them. As a child I roamed barefoot through the fields and bogs and along the streams and rivers. Often I sat in silence for hours, day after day, on a riverbank, alone or with my brothers and sisters or neighbour children, fishing for trout. Silence was part of the rhythm of our lives: we knew the sound of silence and we lived it.

The people I grew up among, many of whom were writers and storytellers, would not have thought of themselves as mystics, but they had a breadth of understanding and a true wisdom that I am sure came from a combination of the life they lived so close to the earth and their long hours of silence as they worked. They had a sense of the sacred that they located not just in church but in the solitude of their own hearts.

Hildegard of Bingen

In early medieval times, around the eleventh and twelfth centuries, there was a group of holy men and women living as hermits in Germany, who were known as the Rhineland mystics. They lived in silence and solitude, and the writings they have left us show a depth of understanding that came not from books or learning, but from their experience of solitude, silence and deep contemplation.

Perhaps the best-known today of these mystics was Hildegard of Bingen (Bingen is a little town on the banks of the Rhine, not far from Cologne), who lived between 1098 and 1179 and may have been Germany's first mystic. She is renowned not only for her sanctity and her writings but especially for the extraordinary religious music she wrote for women's voices, a remarkable achievement for a woman in those times. As well as being a mystic, a visionary, a prophet, a composer and a dramatist, she was a great healer and social reformer and a scientist. Her book of simple medicine is an encyclopaedia of natural science. She also wrote four books on animals, two on herbs and trees, and three on gems and metals, books that are enjoying a new interest in today's world, where we are regaining an interest in natural medicine and holistic healing. She is now recognised for the extraordinary woman she was, with accomplishments in an astonishing range of areas.

Hildegard was particularly close to nature, and acutely aware of the mystery of God's presence in all things. One of my favourite sayings of hers is, 'All creation is a symphony of joy and jubilation.' She wrote extensively about the contrast between night and day, light and darkness, and she was conscious that in the face of our darkness we can touch into our own greatness – the wonder of our own being and the wonder of God.

Hildegard coined the term 'veriditas' (green-ness), which was an expression of nature's power to birth and nurture life. Growing up as she did in the lush verdancy of Rhineland Germany, Hildegard saw a divine presence in her surroundings, and through her contemplation in solitude, she was able to deepen her awareness of the divine presence everywhere. From that verdant landscape in which she lived and contemplated came the metaphors that filled her writing: 'the verdancy of justice', 'the greening power of faith', 'the vigour that hugs the world', phrases that bring to mind Dylan Thomas's poem about the essential unity of humanity and nature: 'The force that through the green fuse drives the flower/Drives my green age.' One of the particular gifts of Hildegard's solitude was the acute perception it gave her of our inter-connectedness with the natural world, and that is a gift that solitude can give anyone who is prepared to receive it.

social solitude

Solitude, which by definition depends on being alone, withdrawing from the company of others, is nevertheless distinct from isolation. By enabling us to be more tuned in to ourselves, solitude in fact allows us to relate to the world around us. Monks and hermits, mystics like Hildegard, live a life of almost total solitude, yet in their way they are vitally linked to the world, although living apart from it. Thomas Merton, a great spiritual thinker and writer, who after an active life in other spheres became a Trappist monk, explained in his writings that the contemplative only withdraws from the world in order to listen more intently to the most neglected voices, which proceed from its inner depths. A monk, he said, is 'a marginal person who withdraws deliberately, with a view to deepening fundamental human experience'.

Solitude is not a form of running away or a refusal to become involved with the world. Rather, solitude helps to create communion, because we take others with us in our hearts into our solitude and there relationships deepen. In solitude we may experience a deep bonding with others, even though we are not present with them at that time.

Solitude and silence make us wise, because in solitude we come to know ourselves, and through this experience we learn to deal more kindly with ourselves and so also with others. Knowing our own struggles, we can recognise the struggles of other people;

knowing our own frailty and fragility we are less quick to condemn, less certain of our convictions and more open to the goodness in other people.

fear of solitude

I believe that in the depth of our hearts we all yearn for solitude, yet at the same time, many of us are constantly trying to escape it. We look at our diaries, with days, weeks, months all filled up and we tell ourselves we don't have the time to spend in solitude. We tell ourselves, 'My work is my prayer' or we may say 'When I finish this work, in a few years, then I'll give more attention to other aspects of my life, I'll make space for myself and for solitude.'

One reason, I think, that we defer a time for solitude, that we don't allow ourselves to make time for it, is that we think it is only by doing things that we can make a difference. We feel that we must have something to show for our good intentions. We feel better if we are doing things for people – cooking them a meal, helping them to get a job, listening to their problems, buying them a gift, whatever it may be. Of course these acts are all very important, but if they become an excuse for feeling ourselves exempt from the need for solitude, then we are doing ourselves a disservice, because we all need solitude and respite from our busy lives.

Another reason we try to avoid solitude may be that we dread loneliness, and so we run hither, thither and yon in a million directions, with an overloaded agenda, always trying to please people, always angry because too much is expected of us and too much remains to be done. But it is a mistake to confuse solitude with loneliness. To be in solitude is to be alone, but it is not to be lonely. Loneliness is the painful experience of being cut off from others or excluded, whereas solitude is an experience of being serene and at peace and free and yet being alone.

We all have lonely moments, moments when we are afraid to be alone, and so to avoid being alone, we keep going, we keep up a wretched pace in our lives, afraid to risk letting ourselves and the world know who we are. We are afraid that if we stop our ceaseless activity, we will not be loved, or we will not be loved enough.

Whatever degree of loneliness we experience and whatever form it takes, it is only when we can accept it and acknowledge it that we can be healed. In solitude, we can confront our loneliness, and confront too the real cause of it.

the voice within

Time spent in solitude is a time to be and to listen without doing and without being busy planning and analysing, theorising, judging. It is a time to be open to the moment, a time to listen with a quiet mind. It is only inside ourselves in solitude that we can begin to hear that 'still small voice within', the voice of our intuitive heart, which can so easily be drowned out in our busy minds.

In his novel, *Siddhartha,* the German mystical writer, Herman Hesse, writes about the wisdom of listening, especially listening to nature, and about the stillness nature brings. He tells us how the disciple learned more from listening to the river than his master Vasudeva could teach him: 'He learned from it continually, and above all he learned from it how to listen with a still heart, with a waiting open soul, without passion, without desire, without judgement, without opinion.' We can only learn to listen like this when we are prepared to stop and be still, to be open and be empty so that we can hear the inner stirrings of our heart and of the heart of the universe.

The more deeply we listen, the more we tune ourselves to the cries of our heart and discover a way of staying with these cries, listening to them and learning to respond to them. The more quiet we become and the more we listen, the more we become aware of the greater consciousness and the greater wisdom of which we are part and which is part of us, and the more we become aware of how inter-connected we are with all of creation and with the creator at work within us.

Our conscious minds can only grasp a very tiny fraction of the reality of our ultimate identity as children of God. In solitude and in silence we can enter a deeper level of consciousness of the inter-relatedness of things, our connections to and essential unity with the universe. In solitude our hearts and minds can be raised to a level of consciousness we cannot possibly attain amid the noise and chatter and clutter of our working lives.

In solitude we are called beyond the limits of our humanity. Solitude gives us space, it distances us from other parts of out life, and this enables us to see things in their true perspective.

finding ourselves in solitude

A time for solitude is a time for intimacy with ourselves, a time to befriend ourselves and embrace ourselves. Intimacy with ourselves is impossible if solitude is not a habit of our lives. Solitude creates the conditions for us to be at home with ourselves, and it is only through being at home with ourselves that we can learn how to be at home with others and with our God.

'The unhappiness of a person resides in one thing: to be unable to remain peacefully in a room,' wrote the seventeenth-century scientist and mathematician Blaise Pascal. But it is not easy to be alone with ourselves, to rest with ourselves in solitude. One reason we tend to shy away from solitude is that we don't want to meet ourselves, we are afraid of who we really are. Solitude brings us face to face with ourselves and we may not like what we see. In solitude our souls are laid bare. In solitude we are made to face our own inner compulsions, how manipulative we are, our mixed motivations for what we do, the way we use people. In solitude, if we are honest with ourselves, we can see what we could be but are not, what we want to be and have failed to become, and there we find a new depth of emptiness in ourselves.

And yet it is also in solitude that we can learn to see beyond those frailties of ours, that emptiness within, to a new depth of potential and a new self-awareness, which leads to self-acceptance. If we reject ourselves, if we refuse to say yes to who we are, then we are impoverishing ourselves. If on the other hand we can accept ourselves as we are, with our faults and inadequacies and, in the silence and solitude of our own hearts, embrace who it is we are, then we can make room for the transforming power of love to begin within us and to radiate through us.

Being alone with ourselves is demanding, yet if we do not learn to face ourselves we will live a life of shallowness. It is in solitude that we can discover the true beauty of ourselves. In solitude we find, deep down inside ourselves, a microcosm of all the hopes and fears, joys and sorrows, pain and delight of the whole universe. Silence and solitude enable us to listen beyond the chaos that is inside us and around us and to hear our own unasked questions.

In solitude we can tune ourselves in to the true source of our being, the true source of our identity and security, which we may call God. It is in solitude that we can face without fear our own inner poverty and our brokenness – our faults, our frailties, our inadequacies – knowing that in God's embrace we are transformed by a love that has no requirements and no limits.

a sacred space

All cultures have had their sacred places and spaces: places in the wild, gardens, cemeteries, cathedrals, monasteries, mosques. Today's people too are seeking space and sanctuary for the sake of their own sanity. We all need this space for solitude and we can all find time for it if we make it a priority, if we value it. We can only value it if we experience it, but once we have experienced it, we will prize the opportunity to stop, reflect, be quiet and feed our spirit, alone and at rest with ourselves.

solitude deepens wonder

I've been lucky enough to visit some of the most extraordinary places on earth and have gazed in wonder at the immensity of the Grand Canyon and watched the staggering magnificence of the sunrise over the Himalayas. But experiences of awe and wonder can occur in much more modest surroundings and at unexpected moments, on coming across a moving poem, for example, or suddenly noticing the first snowdrops of the year.

G K Chesterton once said: 'Wonders will never be lacking in this world of ours; what is lacking is wonderment.' Wonderment, or the ability to wonder at the universe, is a gift, but it is a gift we can miss if we are too busy being busy. It is so easy simply to trudge or zoom through the days and miss the daily gifts of life. I am sometimes startled when somebody mentions a new corner shop that has opened, for example, or an old one that has closed, realising that I hadn't noticed these changes going on around me even though I may pass the place every day going to and from my work. Andrew Harvey, a poet and philosopher, writes: 'If we were really looking at this world, we would be moved a hundred times a day, by the flowers at the side of the road, the people we meet, by all that brings us messages of our goodness and the goodness of all things.' It is only if we choose to be attentive, to notice the small changes around us, that we can learn to relish the taste of life fresh every day and to open our hearts to the wonder of things.

Solitude deepens our capacity for wonder. The more we stop and spend time in solitude, the more see that we are forever being wooed into the wonder of God through the wonders of creation which shout out the wonders of God. At times, and especially if we make space for solitude in our lives, we encounter, maybe just for a fleeting moment, a deep knowing within our being, an experience of being in touch with the wonder of the world and the eternal harmony of the universe which exists beneath all the chaos we experience in our everyday lives. As long as we are full of ourselves, though, with no empty space for solitude and silence, we are incapable of wonderment and life seems empty. But in wonderment we lose ourselves, we are emptied of our little selves and suddenly we realise how wonderful the world is and how full of wonder, how full. It is a strange paradox that the more we forget ourselves, the more we find our true selves.

It is when we stop and take time for silence and solitude that we can learn to be attentive, and attentiveness is a prerequisite for wonderment. If we paid attention to everything we hear, see, smell, touch we would be totally different people. We would be constantly moved to be surprised, to be amazed, to be in a state of wonder and awe.

leisure is a virtue

Time spent in solitude and silence helps us to slow down in the midst of our busy lives, not necessarily so that we do less but so that we do what we do more attentively, more reverently, more leisurely. This leisure is not the privilege of those who have time but the virtue and the wisdom of those who take time to live attentively and to take things as they come, one by one, singling out each person, place, experience and situation and living them to the full. The virtues of leisure and attentiveness allow us to enjoy the journey and not to miss it because we are so concerned with the destination, the result, the product.

I once visited Ithaca, a tiny island off Kapholina in Greece. A local boatman from Kapholina took a few of us there on a daytrip. Even though our visit to the island was very short, I was determined to see the old Byzantine monastery in the hills. As a result of going to look for it, I missed the boat back. Naturally enough, I became very anxious about my situation, separated from my friends, with night beginning to fall. My anxiety to cram so much into the day had caused me to miss the boat, and now my anxiety about my situation prevented me from enjoying the beauty of the island and humanity of the people of the tiny fishing village I found myself stranded in. Eventually, well into the night, the boatman realised he was missing a passenger and he came back for me, but I had missed my opportunity to enjoy my unexpectedly extended stay on the island.

After I returned home I read the poem 'Ithaca' by the Greek poet Constantine Cavafy, which begins: 'When you start on your journey to Ithaca,/then pray that the road is long,/full of adventure, full of knowledge.' I hadn't done that: I had concentrated too much on my destination and failed to enjoy the journey. Here is another verse from that poem:

> *Always keep Ithaca fixed in your mind.*
> *To arrive there is your ultimate goal.*
> *But do not hurry the voyage at all.*
> *It is better to let it last for long years;*
> *and even to anchor at the isle when you are old,*
> *rich with all that you have gained on the way,*
> *not expecting that Ithaca will offer you riches.*
> *Ithaca has given you the beautiful voyage.*
> *Without her you would never have taken the road.*

A TIME TO PRAY

Praised be your name, no one./For your sake/we shall flower/
Towards/you.

PAUL CELAN

Prayer is the spiritual idea that is perhaps most resisted by those who
see themselves as outside of churches or religious traditions. We tend
to think of it as something that very pious – maybe over-pious –
people do, whispering at the back of the church or hunched over
their beads or prayer-books. The way we were brought up may have
encouraged us to believe that the more prayers we say, the better we
are, as if we could measure prayer in terms of words and time. Not
surprisingly, we tend to reject that notion of prayer, based on 'saying
prayers'.

It is essential to distinguish for ourselves between 'saying prayers'
and praying. Prayer doesn't necessarily involve saying anything at all
but rather has to do opening ourselves to the divine and receiving the
outpouring of the divine that is available to us if we but stop and wait
for it. It is not something we do to satisfy God or to pay our prayer

bills. It is rather something we do in response to a deep longing inside ourselves.

Most of us have at some time experienced moments of openness, moments of universal communion, moments of rapturous wonder, moments when we sense a union with something beyond ourselves, moments when we have an overwhelming sense of a limitless belonging. What we sense in those moments is what I call God, and those experiences are in my view moments of prayer. Whether or not we are comfortable with the term 'prayer', most of us are prepared to acknowledge that such moments and such experiences exist for us.

What counts is not the frequency or intensity of these experiences or whether or not we actually call them prayer; what counts is recognising them for what they are – moments when we can drink deeply from the source that gives meaning to our lives.

everyone prays

I contend that there is no human person who does not pray, one way or another, whether formally and consciously or simply in experiencing fleeting or more sustained moments of connection with God.

To pray is to live in communion with the divine. Our human hearts are ever restless in their quest for the divine, and so our hearts have to pray; otherwise they would shrivel up and become hard and we would no longer be truly human. Prayer is being aware of what Yeats calls 'the deep heart's core', and it nourishes our heart with meaning. It is, as Eliot says, 'a condition of complete simplicity'.

Prayer is perceiving the divine in noise and in quiet, in light and in dark, in the poetic and in the mundane, in the play of children and in the faces of the old, in the laughter of the carefree and in the dull eyes of those who are poor or homeless, broken by life, work, or exposure.

Prayer is the divine taking possession of us. We never achieve prayer; it is always received as a gift. If we are prepared to pray, we lift our hearts, souls and minds to the divine, and we develop an attitude of heart that can transform every aspect of our lives. We expose to

God who we are and God gazes on us with the creative and transforming eye of love.

There is a line in an E E Cummings poem that goes: 'I am through you so I.' He doesn't say, I am through you so happy or so alive, but 'so I'. This union of mind and heart that in the Cummings poem is the union of the lover and the beloved can occur also between the person and God, and when it does, we call it prayer.

attentiveness

The great Christian mystic Teresa of Avila described prayer as 'noticing God, noticing us'. Prayer is noticing, being attentive and being aware. It is noticing more keenly what is around us. It is being part of 'the life of things', as Wordsworth put it. It is reading the signs of the times with a new and deepened understanding. Prayer enables us to live freely and gracefully in harmony with the universe. It is seeing, with Aldous Huxley, 'God everywhere, in the living geometry of a flower, a sea shell, an animal, in the love and gentleness, the confidence and humility which give beauty to the relationship between human beings.'

The Christian thinker and teacher Anthony de Mello, whose name is most closely associated for us in the West with the ideas of awareness and attentiveness, drew heavily on the eastern spiritual traditions in his teachings, and particularly on the Zen tradition. One story he liked to tell went like this:

> A disciple asked his master, could there be anything more wonderful than the beauty of creation. For a long time the master was silent. Then he responded, 'Yes, indeed there is.' 'What can this possibly be?' the disciple asked, and the master answered, 'Your own present awareness of the wonders and beauty of creation.'

Awareness is the essence of prayer. In the Zen tradition, mastering awareness is the window to enlightenment. Awareness produces in us a contemplative approach to life, it enables us to see reality with a different eye, it evokes in us the capacity to be filled with wonder and awe. When we are interiorly aware, we are in a state of reverential appreciation.

Prayer happens in attentiveness, because the tuning in to the rhythm of the universe that is prayer takes effort, alertness, wakefulness, attention. To tune in to the whole of creation, to listen to and to hear the music of the universe, to learn the steps of the universal dance, we must listen and respond. In this way, prayer is a powerful, sacred dance with God and the world.

presence

Prayer is about presence and it is about the present moment. In prayer there is no pretence, no control, no glitter, no sham – just presence in heart and mind.

The first steps in the dance of prayer are finding the time and the space to be present. It's not easy, just to be present. We are usually either ahead of ourselves or we are hanging behind. We are either stretching out to a future that has not yet come, or hanging on to a past that is no longer here. We are here in our time, which is the present, and yet we are not here because we are not awake to the reality that the time is now.

Time in prayer is not our time. As Eliot says, it requires a new understanding of time. The Greek word *kairos* is used to express this concept. Kairos is the holy time, the holy moment, the acceptable time, the time that the psalmist talks about when he says, 'Today when you hear his voice, harden not your hearts.' This day, this moment is always and it is now.

Prayer time is not measured by the clock. When we let go of our time, all time is ours and we are the untimed, because we are in the present moment, in the now that transcends time. When it comes to time in prayer we find that there is only a screen between the past and the future and so the now is not in time at all – now is beyond time. The one thing we can be certain of about prayer is that when we are in the presence of God there is no need to hurry and no need to worry. We don't need to plan or think – all we need is to be, to be present, to believe, to love, to listen, because God is breathing on us. God never hurries, is never anxious or pressing, God just waits, breathing gently on us with great tenderness.

wonderment

For me, prayer has two essential ingredients: concentration and wonderment. It is when we combine concentration and wonderment that we are open to God.

Children, even very small ones, are capable of great concentration and absolute determination and absorption when they are playing with their trainset or doll's house or other toys, and at the same time they are full of wonderment and are constantly open to surprise. This is how we must be in order to pray: we must concentrate utterly on our union with God, while being in a state of wonderment. To pray is to allow the child within us to come into its own, constantly ready to be constantly surprised by God.

the practice of prayer

Prayer is never private. Whatever is private excludes someone, but prayer is always an inclusive communion with God and with others. Nevertheless, prayer is spending quality time alone with God, and so it is something we need solitude for, and we need to find the time and space in which to do it.

This takes time and effort. It doesn't happen all by itself. It's facile to say that all life is prayer; our lives can be a continuing prayer, but to say so as if it happens just like that is to miss the true meaning of prayer. All our life is prayer only if we are prayerful people to start with, and to become prayerful people we need to develop the habit of prayer. To do this, we need to develop a disciplined practice of prayer. It is out of that disciplined regular practice that we become prayerful people and it is only then that prayer flows over into everything else in our lives.

Everybody has different ways of making space for prayer in their lives, but I find that it is helpful to allocate particular times for prayer, time I set aside just to be alone with God. That requires discipline but it doesn't have to mean regimentation. Discipline is an attitude that expresses my desire to pray.

I like to pray early in the morning and I like to start with a preparatory ritual. Usually, I take off my shoes, maybe pull back my curtains, even if it is still dark, open the window, water my plants. Then I lay down a mat and light a candle, reminding myself that I am entering into a place and a space where I am alone with myself and my God. The very simple acts of pulling back the curtains and lighting the candle are part of my prayer, because prayer involves realising with my eyes and mind and heart that I am in the presence of the goodness and greatness of God, whatever way that goodness and greatness speaks to me.

I like to start by consciously placing myself in God's presence, realising that prayer is all God's work. Like Denise Levertov, 'I learn to attain freefall and float into creator spirit's deep embrace.' If I find it difficult to quieten down and be present to God, I use my breath to slow down my mind and body, concentrating on my breathing. Sometimes I use a mantra to help me to move into that quiet space within me where I can meet my God in a special way.

When I am at peace in my quiet space, I like to begin by taking a reading from scripture, or maybe another book, whatever I feel drawn to, reading a verse or two to help me to hear what God is saying to me. I let the words or phrases stay with me, and in that quiet time make space for God to speak to me.

I find images helpful. By letting words or phrases from my reading stay with me, I allow an image to emerge from them. Images, I find, help me to stay focused and centred. They can also help me to make connections between the concrete and the intangible, between my inner and outer worlds.

I also like to keep a journal, which I write during or at the end of my prayer time. Writing down my reflections helps me to integrate my life and my prayer.

That is the pattern I tend to follow, but of course everyone finds their own way. I simply offer this account in case it is helpful to other people.

Prayer is God's work: it is a handing over to God. This is how Denise Levertov describes it:

> *I do nothing.*
> *I give You nothing.*
> *Yet You hold me*
> *minute by minute*
> *from falling.*

A TIME TO BE STILL

In stillness a flower blooms, in stillness it fades away.

There is a place in the depth of our being that is protected and saved for ourselves, an inner, sacred space guarded by God's presence. We can all find that still place. Sometimes we only shout into it when we are broken or wounded and empty, but it is in and through that still point that we can find our way into the beauty that transforms us into strong, loving, wise and beautiful people.

The Latin phrase *tranquillitas ordinis* means 'the stillness of order'. It is not a static but a dynamic stillness. It is the candle lighting, the flame burning, moving, but in a calm and orderly way so that to gaze on it stills us. A spinning wheel is the same: it whirls at great speed but about a still centre; similarly, a river is eternally flowing but is nevertheless in the same place. Any of these experiences – contemplating a candle burning steadily, watching a wheel, listening to the river – can help us to enter into our own place of inner peace, where we can find and be at one with ourselves.

Being still is not passive; it is an activity that allows us to live our lives fully. Our everyday lives can often be dulled or overwhelmed by routine and commitments, but if we take time out of the every day to listen without distraction, we become aware of the spirit's movement within us, and we learn to develop a sense of well-being when we make right decisions. Stopping to listen can help us to recognise God within the complexity of our lives. It can also help us when the rhythm of our life shifts and we face new personal, social or spiritual challenges and opportunities.

In the stillness of our being, wisdom guides us to embrace those traits that previously were unknown to us, or that previously we weren't able to face. Meeting ourselves in this way can be disturbing, but once we accept and embrace ourselves, it brings us a peace and a calm we didn't know before – because we discover that, far from being as bad as we feared, we have a great beauty hidden within us, waiting to be explored.

> *Within this earthen vessel are bowers and groves and within it is the creator.*
>
> KABIR

discovering stillness

When Dag Hammerskjöld was head of the United Nations, he established a meditation room in its headquarters in New York City to give diplomats, employees and visitors – regardless of religion – the opportunity to retreat for prayer, meditation and quiet time. He wrote an inspirational text in his own hand and placed it in the room. The first sentence of the text read, 'In each of us there is a centre of stillness surrounded by silence.' By this inner stillness he probably meant what the mystics meant by 'the fine tip of the soul'. He rightly knew that this stillness exists already in each of us – we do not need to create it. All we need do is find the spot where it can be accessed. The path may have been travelled very little by us and it may be overgrown, but it is there if we seek it out. 'Be still and know that I am God,' the psalmist sang.

We all probably know people who radiate this stillness. A woman who cares for elderly people told me recently with gratitude how inspiring she found their deep stillness. 'There is stillness and peace radiated in their eyes and sometimes it is a kind of brightness,' she said.

Etty Hillesum was a thoughtful young Dutch woman, a victim of the Nazi concentration camps. In the diary she kept in the midst of the Nazi occupation, she describes the tender balance between her daily tasks and her deeper search for peace:

> *We have to fight them daily like fleas, those small worries about the morrow, for they sap our energies, the things that have to be done must be done and for the rest we must not allow ourselves to become infested with thousands of petty fears and worries. Ultimately, we have just one moral duty to reclaim large areas of peace in ourselves and reflect it towards others. And the more peace there is in us, the more peace there will also be in our troubled world.*

We are so used to an abundance of words that stillness tends to frighten us. It seems to us like a vast empty space; we look down into its expanse and get dizzy or else we feel a marvellous attraction towards the stillness that leaves us bewildered.

But when we discover stillness, when we take the time each day, even if it is only for five minutes, to close our eyes and to shut away the busyness of our lives, we find that this great emptiness is already filled to the brim with what we cannot even imagine. Divine wisdom awaits us all in stillness and in silence.

> *After he had dismissed them, he went up on a mountainside by himself to pray. When evening came, he was there alone.*
>
> MATTHEW 14:23

Silence and stillness are 'useless' in the sense that, like many of life's most important elements – air, sea, mountains, flowers – we cannot assess their value in monetary terms. We have to learn their usefulness through our experience of our need for them. What is truly necessary will always crave our attention. 'Behold the lilies of the field': here Jesus is inviting us to take time to open ourselves to what appears to be useless, to see things as they really are, and to learn to value them.

joy in stillness

Our time and our culture invariably tells us that actions and accomplishments are better than rest; that doing something, doing anything, is better than doing nothing. And so we go on with our lives and because we do not stop to *be*, to be still, we lose our way and we don't notice the compass points that show us where to go. We bypass sources of nourishment on the way and we miss the silence and stillness that would give us wisdom. We lose the sheer joy and love found in effortless being. Because of the absence of times to *be* in our lives, our lives are diminished.

In our world, success is the legitimate goal of life. In our drive for success, we are seduced by the promises of more: more money, more satisfaction, more recognition, more information, more influence, more love, more possessions, more security. Even when our efforts are sincere and our intentions have integrity, even when we dedicate our lives to others, the sheer pressure of our activity is corrosive and causes sufferings to ourselves and to others. Because of the absence of stillness in our life, we miss out on what makes life fruitful, joyful and happy.

An overactive life can become a violent life, doing violence to ourselves, our homes, our families, our communities. This violence can only be healed by quiet times, silence, time to be still, time for effortless nourishing. When we dedicate time to listen to the small still voice within, we are brought back to and we remember the route of inner wisdom from where we are most deeply nourished and what makes our life fruitful. Without these times, we react from a survival mode where even the smallest thing assumes a huge and terrifying prominence. When we drive a motorbike at high speed, even the smallest pebble on the road can be deadly. So when we are moving faster and faster, every action, every meeting, every encounter takes on a much greater importance and urgency than it really has, and our reaction is equally extreme.

A doctor once told me that when he saw patients when he was tired or overworked, he would order a lot of tests. He said that he was so exhausted he could not tell what was wrong. But when he took time to be and to be still and built it into his day, and took the opportunity to stop between his patients, he could rely on his intuition and his experience to give a pretty accurate diagnosis.

The invitation to stillness is rooted in an undeniable spiritual gravity that allows all things to rest and to settle, to find their place. There comes a moment when more effort actually becomes counter-productive; when our noisy, frantic busyness only muddies the water of our wisdom and understanding. When we become still and allow our life to rest, we feel a renewal of energy and a gradual clarity of perception.

The practice of resting, of being still, restores us. When we allow the cares and concerns of the workplace to fall away, we can simply delight in being alive to savour the gifts and blessings of life and creation. When we act from a place of stillness, we are more capable of having a right understanding, making right judgements and taking right actions.

In stillness we can begin to hear the voice of our intuitive heart, a voice that is drowned to everyday living. But what is even more surprising is that in stillness we can also dissolve the distance between us and others and between us and the whole universe.

mindfulness

Much of modern life is specifically designed to seduce our attention away from our inner place of stillness. The seductions are insatiable.

Hundreds of channels of cable and satellite television and radio, iPods, junk mail and email, interactive Internets, telephones with multiple lines and call waiting, where we can talk to many people at any one time. And on top of that we have billboards, magazines and newspapers. Every stimulus competes for our attention: buy me, do me, watch me, hear me, try me, drink me. If we don't take time out from this world, it can consume us. We all need to disconnect from the frenzy of activity, consumption and accomplishment and consecrate this time to being fully ourselves where we can breathe deeply in the rhythms of life of the earth and of the spirit.

We read in the Bible that God created a world in six days and on the seventh day, God rested. The ancient rabbis teach us that on the seventh day, God created tranquility, serenity, peace and repose, which means rest in the deepest possible sense of fertile, healing stillness. Until the seventh day, creation was unfinished, it was only after the birth of tranquility that the circle of creation was full and complete.

When writer and psychiatrist Scott Peck, who led a very full and busy life, was asked how he could do all he did, he answered 'I can because I spend at least two hours a day doing nothing.' Scott Peck had built into his day time for silence, stillness and meditation. Being still is doing nothing intentionally for a period of time, it may be thirty seconds, sixty seconds or longer. Being still is stopping so you can be awake, so you can pay attention to what is going on both inside and outside. It is close to what the Eastern spiritual traditions call mindfulness.

In the Buddhist Community of Plum village in France where Thich Nhat Hahn the Vietnamese monk resides, mindfulness bells are frequently rung. On hearing a bell, everyone stops and takes three silent mindful breaths. Then they continue their work awakened by the call and the pause of mindfulness. We can choose anything to stop us like this in our day; a telephone ringing, the traffic lights, before we start the car, before we turn the key in the door, before we eat or drink. We can simply stop and take three silent mindful breaths and then answer the phone or turn the knob. We will find that these short still points during the day will change us.

still points

The still point represents the centre, the quiet core where God's spirit dwells in us. Do you know that 'God's spirit dwells in you'? (2 Cor Ch 3 V 16). Sometimes we don't seem to know it. Yet in some holy place within us, God lives and moves and has his being (2 Cor Ch 6 V 16). At this innermost centre of our being, a place where we are deeply and profoundly known and loved by God, is the divine presence in our midst. It is here we attach ourselves to God. It is also where God attaches to us. The still point is an embrace. St Hildegard of Bingen, the great medieval mystic, wrote 'God hugs you. You are embraced by the arms of the mystery of God.' What a wonderful image: God's hug. That circle – the loving embrace with the divine – is our still point. It is where Thomas Merton says 'God has written his name on us.'

Still points during the day create an oasis whereby the turbulent waters caused by the demands of our daily lives are quietened and we can again see our own reflection. Still points are focused, they grow and deepen with practice and they are the backbone of a calm, serene life. Visited regularly, our still points help to make us much more peaceful, more satisfied and more calm. Finding still points in our day does not mean running away from life or avoiding responsibility. On the contrary, it is moving into life and its responsibilities in a new way. Finding still points in our day helps us to bring together the threads of our life, of our story. It helps us remember who we are, where we've come from, where we are going, and where we want to go. It helps us remember why we started doing what we do so that we can see if that is still what we want to do.

Still points are endless; we shouldn't underestimate their power on our life. Stopping during our day for a minute or two can be full of meaning and power. We can at that particular moment remember that we are in the presence of the divine and that God's grace is available to us right here and now. As Rumi the poet writes, 'Everything you want and need is inside you,' and elsewhere he writes, 'You have a source inside you, a cool spring.'

Robert Frost in his poem, 'Stopping by Woods on a Snowy Evening', gives us a wonderful example of stopping or being still. He does nothing but stop and watch the woods fill up with snow. He is awake and aware of his surroundings, his aloneness in the woods and the absence of a landowner. He just sits quietly in the falling snow, he feels the woods and names them 'lovely, dark and deep'. Then he remembers, 'I have promises to keep and miles to go before I sleep.' We can assume he returns to his life and whatever he was doing when he stopped to watch, now refreshed by his stopping.

When I'm giving a lecture, I can be still ten times or more during the presentation. I can take a deep breath, focusing and reminding myself what I am doing, what I want to create in this lecture, what I want to offer the participants and then go back to what I am doing. This only takes ten seconds or so and the participants experience it only as a brief pause. These times are life's little golden moments when, taken together, can bring brilliance and joy to otherwise dull days. What we do during these times is very simple – we stop doing whatever we are doing, we sit or stand, take a deep breath with our eyes open or closed. We may be on a bus, we may be on a train or on a plane, at the kitchen sink, on the phone or at the computer, and we begin by simply noticing our breathing, focusing our attention inward and remembering what we need to remember; our hopes, our beliefs, what motivates us. It can be reciting a mantra, maybe remembering a prayer for strength for peace or remembering somebody important to us. Or it may be simply smiling softly. Having still points in our day makes a huge difference to us, especially if we practise it regularly and intentionally.

The German poet Rainer Maria Rilke also talks about the importance of stillness in many of his poems. In *The Book of Hours*, he writes:

> *I am the rest between two notes.*

The poet invites us to be like him – a rest between two notes, that brief, measured moment between the time when one note of music stops and another begins. Without that rest, it would be a chaotic racket. All notes and no rest would be a babel, the sound would not be music, it would be more like a siren. Being still makes the space between the notes important.

When the American naturalist Henri David Thoreau decided to go and live at Waldon Pond, away from the hustle and bustle of city life, he said:

> *I went to the woods, because I wanted to live deliberately to front only the essential facts of life and see if I could not learn what is there to teach and not when I came to die discover that I had not lived.*

Most of us can't retire to the woods, but we can create the Waldon moments for ourselves by making space and time in our days for still points. Thoreau writes about what it was like to 'live deliberately' and gives a wonderful description of the still points when he says, 'I sat on my sunny doorway from sunrise till noon wrapped in reverie.' He tells us how he grew, 'I grew in those seasons as a corn in the night.' If we just imagine for ourselves what it's like being inside a cornstalk, being inside the growing ear, absorbing the nutrients from the earth, having retained in our flesh the warmth of the day's blazing sun, drinking in the moisture of the dew, and combining it all to create the miracle of the bright, yellow food. That is how we grow in the still points. It happens on its own. We don't have to do anything.

Lao-Tzu says, 'The way to do is to be'. Still point is doing nothing to become more fully awake and remember who we are. We all need to discover our own unique paths, the ways, the times, the places, the triggers, the occasions and the opportunities to be still by just watching what is going on, falling snow, setting sun, growing grass or whatever is close to us.

A TIME FOR SIMPLICITY

In the 1950s, a woman who called herself Peace Pilgrim began a walk across America to promote her vision of peace. Before setting off on her journey, she pared down her possessions to what she felt were the essentials – the clothes she was wearing on her back and a few items in her pockets. She found that living with only the most basic things both liberated and empowered her, and she rejoiced in the freedom this choice gave her. When she was asked why she chose to live so simply, she replied: 'A persistent simplification will create an inner and outer well-being that places harmony in one's life.'

There are many advantages to living a simpler, harmonious life. Simplicity clears our vision and allows us to see what we really need as well as what really qualifies as enough. Simplicity frees us from the false values that rank possessions and endless striving above all else. Simplicity releases old attachments so that we can free ourselves from the past and live more fully in the present. Simplicity reduces the daily confusion and restores order in our life. It shifts us away from a search for security that comes from things outside ourselves –

things that become an emotional crutch and provide an illusion of security – and turns us to look instead within ourselves to our own sense of peace and harmony.

The seventeenth-century theologian and poet Angelus Silesius wrote: 'One has not lived in vain who learns to be unruffled by loss, by gain, by joy, by pain.' Simplicity restores our wholeness, improves our mental health, reduces tension, decreases pollution and increases our sense of community. It brings greater beauty into our lives and moves us closer to nature.

Clutter, on the other hand, throws us off balance when we let it take over our minds or our emotions. We all have a tendency to clutter. Thomas Merton wrote: 'Our minds are like crows, they pick up everything that glitters no matter how uncomfortable our nests get with all that metal in them.' It seems to me that I am forever trying to get rid of the clutter in my life. I have my wastepaper basket emptied, and it is full again. I clear my desk, but the following day it is messier than ever. I tidy my room, I put things away, but it always seems as though there is a stack of something waiting to be sorted and discarded.

Anything can be clutter if it keeps us totally absorbed in ourselves and unaware of what life is offering us. Even very wonderful things like beauty and books and knowledge and pleasure can become clutter when we seek these things at any cost, obsessed with having more. These good things are not bad, but we need to keep them from taking over our life.

Other things, like anxiety, resentment, harsh judgements, self-pity and mistrust, can also take over our spiritual life. Inner voices – negative thoughts, useless fears and worries, old wounds, the should's and the should not's – also control us and squeeze out the good things that are waiting for us.

Negativity is a great clutterer. It can keep us from receiving the joys of the moment, the joy of the day. Somewhere there is a squirrel in each of us, hoarding, preserving, hiding against the unseen winters of life.

Consumerism also contributes to that clutter. Consumerism plays with our minds as we are daily barraged with media messages attempting to convince us that we will be happy only if we have a certain product. Our competitive society drives us into a mode of seeking to have more than or better than others, implying that having more or being 'better' will make us complete and whole. It is this addictive enticement that deters us from grappling with the deeper questions and challenges of simplicity.

Most of us have too much in life; too many clothes which jade our appreciation for new ones; too much money which can remove us from reality; too much free time which can dull the edge of our soul. Sometimes we need to regain our balance, to go very near the bone so that we can taste the core and marrow of life, not just its superfluities.

For many of us, our daily busyness is part of the clutter as well – we keep ourselves constantly engaged in noise and activity so we don't have to sit with the truth in our heart. We cling on to past relationships, events and memories by accumulating items associated with them – to avoid our fear of letting go, of engaging with the truth and moving on into the future. Clutter is endless and we all have our own patterns of accumulation and avoidance.

accepting ourselves

'We own only what can't be lost in a shipwreck,' the Arab proverb teaches. This image is startling and all the more so because it is true.

A simplified life is an accepted life, and accepting ourselves is probably the hardest of all. Accepting our own giftedness, as well as our less-than-perfect selves, is one of the biggest hurdles that we need to face in order to mature spiritually. While it is essential for us to grow into more loving persons, it is equally important for us to accept ourselves as we really are.

Simplicity is like a muscle, it needs to be exercised, worked and stretched. Practising simplicity often requires that we shed many layers of falsehood before coming to the centre of our truth. Many of us have become so controlled with the 'right' ways to think, act, live and believe that we can easily lose touch with the truth that is truly ours. Some of these layers may have been with us for a long time, even from our childhood. We may have been told, for example, that there is only one way to do something or to think and we may have been discouraged from exploring other options. It may be a fear of being unacceptable, or a desire to please others or earn their love, that has led us to question or doubt our own truth. The expectations of our family or of our society may have made it difficult for us to trust the voice of our heart.

Sometimes we become too comfortable with these falsehoods, often fooling even ourselves. A simplified life is one that is comfortable with being. Being helps us to develop awareness, to focus more keenly on our inner activity without needing to do anything except be attentive.

When I give myself to being, when I give myself to attentiveness, I find I discover God everywhere. I hear connections with my deeper life; in music, in correspondence, in telephone calls, in the people I meet, in what I read and touch and taste and in the insights and emotions that arise within me.

Simplicity is expansive, leading us outward beyond ourselves. It connects us with a larger presence of fullness, reflected in our universe, all of which mirrors the immensity of the divine. As we consciously develop and practise the discipline of simplicity, we are challenged to look with eyes that recognise the greatness of the universe, the greatness of God. There's a beautiful Jewish prayer called *Dayenu* which is used at the Passover. This prayer recognises all that we have been given:

> *Had He (God) simply delivered us from Egypt*
> *and not set us on our way, Dayenu!*
> *(That would be enough!)*
> *Had He (God) set us on our way,*

Crossing with us the barrier of the sea,
And not led us through the wastelands, Dayenu!
(That would be enough!)
Had He (God) cared for us during our wanders through the
wastelands
And not ordained us for the Sabbath, Dayenu!
(That would be enough!)
Had He (God) ordained us on the Sabbath
And not brought us to Sinai, Dayenu!
(That would be enough!)

Simplicity has to do with honesty, authenticity and integrity. We live a simple life when we do not pretend to be something we are not. The purely simple person lives a life that is perfectly at ease with themselves. They are not seduced by titles or masks to protect them from the truth about themselves. The truly simple person lives with dignity, whatever life brings them.

With a society that thrives on image and advertising and status, the simple person knows their own inherent worth and value as a human being. They know where they have come from and where they are going. The truly simple person seeks for the essence of life rather than grasping after its frills, whatever shapes these might take in our various worlds. True simplicity grows from an awareness that we can in fact believe and accept that we are unconditionally loved by God, just as we are. When we know that, we can dare to be honest with ourselves and with others.

When we lead a simple life, we can define the essentials in our life. We can freely choose to graciously let go of the non-essentials and clutter in our hearts. We can rest with confidence in the promise of our God who tells us that we will be given all we need. We can do that because we know that emptiness makes way for fullness. To unclutter our lives is to open our hearts to create an emptiness where fullness becomes possible.

Clay is moulded into vessels, and because of the space where there is nothing, you can hold water. Space is carved out from a wall, and because of the space where there is nothing, you can receive light. Be empty, and you will remain full.

LAO TSU

now is the time

This moment can be the beginning moment for each of us as we resolve to live our life more simply. Today we can give away something we treasure which would enrich the life of somebody else and liberate ours. We can discard those things we no longer use by recycling what we can and donating other items to charities. We can decide to seek periods of silence, times in which we shut off the sensory overload that often fails us; from stereos, radios, televisions, iPods, telephones and mindless talk and chatter. We can decide to spend some time alone; thinking, praying, reflecting, reading, exercising, writing or walking, listening to birdsong or smelling the flowers. We can decide today to mediate on a regular basis.

We can decide to use our time more wisely today and live in a harmonious and simple way, knowing that this will bring with it an inner and outer well-being, that radiates peace and joy in our world.

A TIME TO LOVE

There is in all of us, at the centre of our lives, a tension, an aching, a yearning in the heart that is insatiable and very deep. Sometimes this longing is focused in a person, at other times the yearning is a longing to attain something; most often, though, it is a longing without a clear name or a focus. We only know that we are restless, we are full of disquiet, we are aching at a level that we cannot seem to get at.

We can try to fill this 'immortal longing' in ourselves with things; we can clutter it up; or we can recognise it for what it is, the wound of love, the longing in each of us for the immortal, for the divine. Human beings are not perfect; we are incomplete. Our incomplete nature springs towards its own perfection, which we may call God, and we cannot rest until we find the source of our love.

We tend to think of love as some impossible romantic dream. On the contrary, love is not only possible, it is in truth the only reality. Deep within each of us, there is a fountain or a well of love. The greatest gift we can bring to another is to open up to them their hidden reservoir of love. When we do that, when we open up to people their ability to love, we are doing the work of God, and we are freeing people in a way that they didn't know they could be free.

Love is more than a thought and a desire. Love is action. According to the eastern poet and philosopher, Kahlil Gibran, 'Work is love made visible.' It is only in the action of love that we attain the wisdom of love. Only God's love is perfect and truly unconditional. Human love can only approximate that love. Yet if we consent to love and give ourselves over to love in its fullness, then the entire world will be overflowing with love. The first step to attain that openness to love is to admit that our love, even though it isn't perfect, is none the less love and that by virtue of its very nature it aspires to the fullness of love.

the touch of love

Life is filled with invitations to delight in love. It invites us to open our eyes and to look at the world around us so that we can recognise that the festive meal is right in front of us, the banquet of love with wine and food, that unbeknownst to us it is within our reach.

Plato said, 'At the touch of love, everyone becomes a poet,' and certainly the poets and the artists never tire of depicting love. Neruda wrote: 'I want to do with you what the spring does with the cherry trees.' When we love, we recognise a depth in the presence of the other that cannot be seen or found without love. Yeats speaks of a 'little space for the rose breath to fill'. Love is being able to recognise the uniqueness and the special nature of the other, to allow the energy of creativity to flow.

We look to one that we love for tender support and tough truth. We find our worth in the one we love, in their attention, interest, care and concern. We find in their look that we are attractive, we find in their laughter that we are engaging, and in their responses that we have something of value to say. We find in them somebody who respects our gifts, especially the gifts we have difficulty in seeing in ourselves. Love sees the little good that is in us and forgives everything that is not good. Love gives meaning to life. It is the bridge, the survival, the meaning that 'links', as Wilder says, 'the land of the living and the land of the dead'.

When we love, our love not only goes out to the person we love, but it goes further and further. It goes out from us and encircles more and more people and the cumulative effects of our love we will never know. We send out vibes of love to people, through what we say and what we do, through what we are and how we love. What we give out comes back to us, because if we love we become loving people and people in turn love us. In other words, we are changed when we love. To be loved is an incredibly precious thing. It is to awaken in the other and to have awakened in us that resource that frees the vast possibilities within us.

Love is a wholehearted *yes* to belonging. When we fall in love, our sense of belonging is overpowering, our *yes* is spontaneous and blissful. It is the sense of belonging that true love can give us that makes us reach out to all, knowing that all belongs to all. When we speak of the heart, we speak of the whole person, for only in heart are we whole. The heart stands for the centre of our being, where we are at one with ourselves, one with all others, and one with that pure spirit of love that some of us call God.

life without love

We are capable of loving our fellow human beings freely, spontaneously; or we can choose to reject and despise them. If we choose this course, our love has turned against our own selves, it has become adulterated, contaminated. That love turns in upon ourselves and is locked up inside ourselves. The love which could and should give nourishment to others consumes us.

Unless we allow our love to grow and develop and flow, it becomes hardened. This is what the prophet Ezekiel was talking about when he spoke of 'our hearts of stone'. Through a lack of love, everything hardens. There is nothing as empty or as cold or as lonely in the world as a heart that has grown hard and embittered.

Without love we limp through life and lack heart and soul. The loss of a loved one is a gap in the heart forever. Nothing replaces it, because a door in one's own life closes that can never be opened by anyone else again.

the pain of love

Love requires a meeting of equals. Those who love grow in love, together and separately. As Kahlil Gibran says of marriage: 'Let there be spaces in your togetherness; let the winds of the heavens dance between you.'

No matter how close we get to another, we are always separate: you can never know what it is like to be me and I can never know fully what it is like to be you. Although we share moments of oneness, when our beings touch, complete union remains just out of our reach. The closer we are the more painful it is; even a hair's breadth of a distance between us seems like a huge ravine. That is part of the pain of love.

Love as we know it – the love of the creature for the earth, the love of the lover for the beloved, the love of the mother for her child, the love of the friend for his friend – is a glimpse of the eternal love of God. It is the only means on earth to get a glimpse of the love of God, which is at the heart of creation. When we really love someone else, with a love that is total and a love that is true, then we have an inkling of how God loves us. It is God's love being revealed on earth. It is almost breathtaking. It is almost unbearable. It is heartbreaking.

Love connects us to the rest of the world. Once we have loved someone, we are freed from ourselves. To love is to see beyond ourselves and it takes trust and commitment and wisdom. And it hurts. In his book *Grace and Grit,* Ken Wilber describes the death of his young wife in these words:

> She moved towards me, trying to gesture, trying to say something, trying to say something that she wanted me to understand… I knew she was aware of how I felt. But my throat was closed in on itself, I couldn't speak. I wasn't crying, I just couldn't speak… Treya closed her eyes and, for all purposes, she never opened them again. My heart broke… I kept on thinking that if love does not shatter you then you do not know love. We had both been practising the wound of love, and I was shattered. Looking back on it, it seems to me in that simple and direct moment we both died.

loving ourselves

We can never love truly love another person, unless we are equally involved in loving ourselves. 'I thank you that I am so wonderfully made,' prays the psalmist, 'I thank you for the mystery of my being.' But most of us have not dwelt on the mystery of our own being. We take ourselves for granted, because we take what is familiar for granted. We go on, day in, day out, doing more or less the same thing, behaving in more or less the same way, and don't plumb the depths of our being; we don't enter into the deep mystery that awaits with us; we reduce the mystery to the ordinary. Yet all the while we are being shaped and reshaped by God, and behind the ordinary lies extraordinary mystery unexplored, extraordinary potential underdeveloped, extraordinary beauty unknown, extraordinary possibilities and blessing and giftedness unknown and unloved.

We are all strangers to ourselves until we stand aside and allow the unknown, the stranger to emerge. Standing on the edge of the unknown self, we do not know what wildness, madness, strangeness might emerge. We like to stay with the familiar, with what we can tame and control, with what we have accepted as us and what is acceptable as us. But it is precisely because we stay with this version of ourselves that the great mystery and beauty of our being never surfaces or emerges and is unknown even in ourselves.

The journey of self-knowledge and self-acceptance is a journey to finding our true selves, to finding and accepting the great mystery of ourselves. In his inaugural speech, Nelson Mandela spoke about this great mystery of our true selves and our fear of it:

> *Our deepest fear is not that we are inadequate; our deepest fear is that we are powerful beyond measure. We ask ourselves, 'Who am I to be brilliant, gorgeous, talented and fabulous?' Actually, who are you not to be? You are a child of God. We are born to manifest the glory of God that is within us. It is not just in some of us: it's in everyone.*

Whether we put it in a religious context or not, what we are called to is to live life to the full, to fulfil our own potential. So we must look within and outside ourselves first to find ourselves and not expect to find the full truth unless we continue each day to search, to seek what we are being called to. This is the struggle of a lifetime, accepting the me within whom lies great beauty and great possibilities, my neglected and ignored dreams of greatness.

One of the problems we have in knowing and loving ourselves is that we can confuse our identity, who we are, with what we do. We tend to define ourselves by what we do, by what we can achieve, rather than by who we are. This makes it hard for us to be open to the mystery of ourselves or to know our true selves. It is also a very risky business, because as we discover more and more of our own true selves we have to let go of our false selves, the ego self, the old crutch, and allow the unknown self to emerge.

Of course we are not perfect. In loving ourselves, we must face the fact that there is a weakness or woundedness or fragility or incompleteness in ourselves. We must accept the shadow side of ourselves. True self-knowledge lays bare the fact that each of us is part light and part darkness, part angel and part monster. It is precisely at the point of acceptance of our fragility and our brokenness that true development and growth can take place. The only possible way of changing is to accept that we are not complete. As Anne Lamott says, 'Hope begins in the dark. The stubborn hope that if you just show up, and try to do the right thing the dawn will come. You wait and watch and work, and you don't give up.'

If we try to stop and meet and accept our own pain and our own frailty, the parts of us that are still incomplete, the part of us that empty us and fragments us, we discover they can be sources of our growth.

We come from God full of brightness and beauty and God is still at the centre of our being. We can go for many years with our beauty unknown and unaccepted by us. But if we stop and listen to our deepest selves, we can grow to our full selves as God's work of art, daughters and sons of God. When we are truly human and truly ourselves, it is God's glory that shines through us.

A TIME TO TAKE A
FRESH LOOK

What is – this life
If, full of care
We have no time
To stand and stare?

WH DAVIES

After spending a year in the United States in the early 1990s, I
returned to Ireland and went on a visit home to Dingle for a week or
so. The first day I was in town, walking down the Main Street in
Dingle, I was greeted as a long-lost friend by a middle-aged couple.
They said they hadn't realised I had returned from America, and we
chatted for a while about my time away and other things. All during
the conversation, which lasted for about twenty minutes, I was trying

to work out who they were. It wasn't just that I couldn't recall their names; I couldn't place them at all.

Just as we were about to part, I had to own up, so I said: 'You know, I'm sorry, but I just can't place you.' They roared laughing at that and replied of course I couldn't place them, because I didn't know them at all, they were from another part of the country, and had just recognised me and stopped to talk. We had a good laugh at my embarrassing few moments, and the conversation continued for a bit, and then as we finally said our goodbyes, the gentleman remarked: 'I bet you didn't meet anyone in Berkeley who stopped on the street for as long as this to have a chat with you.'

He was dead right. Not only did people not chat on the street, but they raced past each other as if the last train was leaving for the gold rush. The only people I met out there who had time to talk were the homeless people, mainly black and sometimes disabled men, who sat on the sidewalks and begged or slept or sang to themselves or made comic remarks to the people passing by.

The Main Street in Dingle certainly has a very different atmosphere from the streets of Berkeley, California, but I know perfectly well that, like anyone with a busy life and a full appointments diary, I wouldn't have had time for this meandering conversation myself, only that I was on holidays, and so were the people I met that day in Dingle. But that little incident did make me think about how important it is to be able to take time sometimes just to stop and make idle conversation, to listen to people, to exchange cordial greetings, to talk just for the sake of talking, with no agenda, to enjoy an encounter just for its own sake. Moments like those are a gift, unexpected, bringing the warmth of human contact, uncontaminated by self-interest or calculation, just a gratuitous little interlude of conversation exchanged.

greetings

That Dingle encounter was a leisurely one that lasted some time, but it was really a sort of extended greeting, a small celebration of a shared humanity, an exchange between people as a token of goodwill. All cultures have greeting rituals, some more elaborate than others, all designed to allow people to honour each other. The European handshake is exchanged particularly when people meet for the first time or if they haven't seen each other for a while. The Japanese bow to each other when they meet. When they enter each other's houses, Hispanic people hang back for a moment in the doorway, waiting to be invited to step in, and say 'Con su permisso' ('With your permission'), thus honouring the space of the other person. The Germans greet each other at midday with 'Gute Mahlzeit' ('Good meal time') or simply 'Mahlzeit,' like a sort of grace at one remove.

The Irish greetings 'Go mbeannaí Dia thú' ('God bless you') and 'Bail ó Dhia ar an obair' ('God bless the work') are more than greetings: they are quite explicitly blessings. These are Christian greetings, but they reflect a Celtic spirituality, which Ester de Waal describes like this: 'The Celtic approach to God opens up a world in which nothing is too common to be exalted and nothing so exalted that it cannot be made common.'

Human greeting practices are ritualised ways of reaching out to and receiving each other. Sometimes the ritual has crystallised to the point where we are hardly aware of what we are saying or doing when we greet each other, but if we take the time to be aware of our greetings, maybe to vary them or extend them occasionally as the couple I met that day in Dingle did, they can be refreshed in us and become a way for us to open our hearts and to see with a new eye.

rainbow moments
It's hard for people who live in a world that bears increasingly more resemblance to my Californian experience than to my Dingle street encounter to make time for extended greetings like that, or to make time simply to stop and stare and enjoy the wonder of the world. That's because in the frenzied way we live today, there isn't much room for the unscheduled encounter, and yet we can draw much sustenance and refreshment from those very encounters, unexpected as they are.

Encounters like those are rainbow moments. Rainbows are a gift. They come quite unexpectedly, apparently from nowhere, and they can capture our attention in a way that almost no other natural phenomenon can. Somebody suddenly looks out the window and points to the sky, saying, 'Look! Do you see the rainbow?' And everyone looks and everyone wonders and everyone is surprised. A rainbow is an invitation to stop and stare.

When we can enjoy moments like that, we are learning to live in the present moment, with an open heart. Living with an open heart means being aware of the now. The present moment is finite: if we anticipate it, that changes it. But when we consent to stop and live in the present moment, without harking back to the past or straining forward to the future, something extraordinary takes place within us. We become conscious of two things. The first is that each moment is the only moment we are sure of, the only moment within which we are asked to live. And the second is that God is radically present now, always now: God is only as close as the present moment.

Our life lasts only a moment, and the challenge to us is to live that moment. The problem is that it is difficult to live always in the present. Our minds are in a constant state of flux. No thought, no feeling, no sensation, it seems, lasts for more than an instant before it is changed into or changed by the next state, thought, or sensation, and that in turn is changed again. With minds like this, it is very difficult to live in the creative tension between the 'now' and the 'not yet', between what is and what might be. We can only do this by making a conscious effort to stop and stare and look afresh, by entering deliberately into the present moment.

polishing the mirror

The best way I know to learn to live in the present moment is to take the time, quite deliberately, to notice and acknowledge the various states and thoughts that pass through our minds, to watch the process of our minds unfolding, moment by moment, thought by thought, feeling by feeling. If you take even five minutes in the day and deliberately focus your attention inwards and then try counting how many states of mind come and go within that five minutes, you will probably be amazed at what you discover. At first you may not notice so many, but if you are faithful to the practice you will start to notice literally hundreds of subtle changes in those five minutes.

Gradually, you can increase the amount of time you spend deliberately focusing on the present moment, and eventually it will become something that you'll find yourself doing all day. This practice of noting our states of mind as they arise keeps us present to the moment. In the Zen tradition, this is called 'polishing the mirror'. The greater our consciousness of each moment, the more we can begin to let go of the stories that control our behaviour and consequently we can develop greater clarity and better vision.

Learning to practise this living in the present moment is a slow process and it can be a daily struggle to do it, but once you move into it and make it part of how you live, it brings extraordinary peace.

surprised by joy

As we open ourselves to the gift of the present moment we take on a new way of seeing: we learn to see with the heart instead of with the mind. Our minds make a lot of assumptions, and these assumptions can distort reality. The less we assume, the more we are surprised and delighted with what we discover in the world.

Occasionally, when we least expect it, a grace comes to us, and like Wordworth we are 'surprised by joy'. A fresh eye looking at the ordinary is the greatest surprise of all. The surprise of the unexpected will wear off, but the surprise of freshness never wears off.

When we live in the now, life is full of freshness: for us then, 'There lives the dearest freshness/Deep down things' as Gerard Manley Hopkins put it. That freshness that Hopkins talks about is what the great religions of the world have all recognised in one way or another as a divine energy at the heart of things, what the Tao calls 'grace' and what the great medieval Christian mystic Meister Eckhart calls 'isness'.

When we are seeing with the heart, we discover that there is no part of life that doesn't contain a surprise. Nothing is too simple or small, nothing is too mundane, nothing is too ecstatic or exalted, nothing is too ordinary or extraordinary – all of life becomes full of potential, full of surprise.

But freshness is, paradoxically, an acquired perception. We have to train ourselves to see it, like E E Cummings, we have to be able to say 'the eyes of my eyes are opened' if we want to see with that fresh eye, that ability to see things anew, as a child sees them.

When we have developed the ability to live in the present moment, when we have learned to take time to see with a fresh eye, then celebration becomes a way of life for us. We recognise and accept and greet each person we meet. Oppression of ourselves or others has no place in our mindset. Compassion becomes the foundation of our attitude to others, as we see them, steadily, with a fresh gaze and an open heart.

A TIME FOR GRATITUDE

The mystic Meister Eckhart preached that if the only prayer we ever said was 'Thank You', it would be enough.

The essence of gratitude is acceptance of what is. It is amazing how we can miss so much of life when we loose our sensitivity to wonder and awe. When we simply drudge through our days, we may easily miss the daily gifts of life, and lose sense of gratitude. On the other hand, when we awaken to what is within us and around us, when we savour, relish and taste life fresh each day, our heart holds much more gratitude.

If we remember the people who have blessed our life, many of them may be unaware of what they have done. They may have blessed us with their smiles, their loving looks, their affirmations, their stories, their love, their compassion, their concern and their care. When we become aware of the vast goodness around us and the great blessings that abound, we also become aware of our own need to bless, with our presence, our goodness, our strengths, our healing, our courage, our vitality.

It is often through tragedies or disasters that we can learn something of life's priority. It is when we have lost somebody or some great treasure or something we have really valued or some irreplaceable possession that we can reach the realisation that life alone is essential. Disasters and tragedies and traumas can be great equalisers, they can give the opportunity for true humility and gratitude to creep in, the gratitude for simply being alive.

moments of grace

Ralph Emerson wrote, 'Never lose the opportunity of seeing anything that is beautiful, for beauty is God's handwriting – a wayside sacrament.'

Vincent Van Gogh once said 'The best way to know God is to love many things.' I find that as I get older, there are numerous opportunities for me to be grateful. This is not the time to moan about how old I am getting nor is it the time to grieve for my lost youth. This is a time to celebrate and be grateful for having come this far. To be grateful that I am more able than ever to enjoy relationships, memories and recollections. That I am able to have perspective on myself and the world, and to enjoy more quiet moments alone. That I am able to give more attention to the inner journey which is the longest journey of all.

Because my life has deepened over the years and has evolved a rich inner vitality made up of memory, insight and confidence, it is now time to appreciate all this and to be grateful. This is a wonderful gift.

I have worked with the poor for over forty years now, and they have taught me many things, but above all, they have taught me to be grateful. They point out all the good things that have been given to us, and how much we take them for granted.

A group of people I know and live among include many who have experienced homelessness, poverty, depression and exclusion.

Over the years, I have had the privilege of sharing with them prayers, liturgies and rituals. What strikes me more than anything else is the extraordinary way in which this group is able to name and claim the moments of grace and gratitude in their lives. They are not calculating or doing cost/benefit analyses of their lives; they are simply acknowledging and recognising and being grateful for everything they have. Together, we are setting down small islands of hope, of celebrations, to help us keep sight of God's great love. During these liturgies and rituals, I realise very clearly that grace comes to us when we begin to appreciate the goodness that is already ours. Even if what we possess does not include many material goods, as we experience gratitude the goods expand and so does our sense of gratitude. Together we are able to acknowledge moments of gratitude for people who walked with us through life, for those who stood beside us when our hopes were small, for those who walked with us when we had nothing but sorrow and death, for those who celebrated our emptiness, for those who broke bread with us and shared with us new life.

Gratitude and greed are mutually exclusive. Greed arises from the belief that we are in control, and that we can control everything, and that anything we have we deserve. Greed is a mindset that tells us we must get and get and get. It is the yearning for more, the push to acquire more, win more, own more, have more. Greed does not know the meaning of enough. Those who lack gratitude's vision do not possess things, things possess them and that is misery. On the other hand, gratitude flows from a vision of one's life as a reality received, a gift given freely and spontaneously.

The poet Rilke, observing the way the anemone flower opens to the morning light, asks, 'When are we ever fully open to receive?' Openness in this sense stands for a basic attitude towards life for a readiness to receive life to the full. This openness is in itself fullness, it is gratitude.

A friend of mine said to me recently, 'I know the sunsets are for everyone, but I believe that what each of us receives from a sunset is a personal gift that is uniquely ours.' I was very moved by her words and it became clear to me that so much depends on whether or not we face life with eyes of gratefulness. If instead we face life with a sense of entitlement, we make demands, set expectations and create rules regarding what we need to be joyful and happy. This sense of entitlement is one of the major enemies to spiritual growth; it hardens our souls and keeps us from appreciating the gifts we have all been given. A demanding nature can even hurt the very people in our lives who may be offering gifts to us. It's all about receiving and not taking. There is plenty for all of us – for you and for me – if only we have the eyes to see and the ears to hear and the heart to feel the gifts all around us and within us.

The way to heal a greedy, envious, or demanding heart is to replace it with a grateful heart. When gratitude becomes our way of life, we make peace with our greed and with our envy, not excusing it or ignoring it, but acknowledging it as part of ourselves. Then with the psalmist we can pray:

> *It was you who created my innermost being, and put me together in my mother's womb. For all these mysteries, I thank you for the wonder of myself and for the wonder of your works.*

Ps. 129:13–14

One of the purposes of prayer is to remind us of the gracious generosity of God and to awaken in us a sense of appreciation for the goodness that is already ours. Prayer moves us deeply into the mystery of grace, and prayer opens us to the abundance of God. Here our emptiness becomes a gift rather than a disappointment, as God fills us with love. The more empty we are, the more we know our need for God. And in humility we begin to recognise the gifts and graces bestowed on us over our lifetime.

thanksgiving

Gratitude is not just a feeling. It is not enough to feel grateful – we must think grateful, imagine grateful and act grateful. We cannot simply say 'Thank You' and then continue in a demanding, controlling or competitive way. Gratitude is a whole and holy attitude.

Gratitude is at the heart of a healthy spirituality. When we are grateful, our lives will begin to change instantly and we will see that we have so much more that we previously realised, even during those times when the world would have us think we are poor.

Sometimes we find it hard to be grateful for something, because we have difficulty in acknowledging a gift; because when I admit that something is a gift, I admit my dependence on the giver. There is something within us that bristles at the idea of dependence. We want to get along by ourselves, yet a gift is something we simply cannot give to ourselves, not as a gift at any rate. I can buy the same thing or even something better, but it will not be a gift if I procure it for myself.

This dependence is always there when a gift is given and received. Even a mother depends on her child for the smallest gift. Even though she has given him not only the money he spent on the gift, but his very life and the upbringing that made him generous.

In the past, people expressed their thanks by saying, 'I am much obliged.' We hardly ever hear people saying that today, and that is because people don't want to be obliged, don't like acknowledging their dependence on other people.

The greatest gift we can give is thanksgiving. In giving gifts, we often give what we can spare, but in giving thanks, we give ourselves. The one who says 'Thank you' to another really says 'We belong together'. The giver and the thanksgiver belong to each other. The bond unites them and frees them from alienation.

Gratitude helps us to keep perspective and make connections that might otherwise be overlooked. Gratitude is like the sun lighting up the landscape, not a single leaf or blade of grass is different but everything looks much more attractive. People who are grateful can maintain a playful attitude and can laugh at themselves and reduce anger and annoyance. Gratitude helps us to see things in relative terms, to see the proper relationship between things more readily. Gratitude is indispensable on the way to maturity; it dignifies and celebrates life and presumes trust.

Towards the end of his brief life, Dag Hammarskjöld wrote, 'The night is closing in. For all that has been, thanks, for all that is to come, yes.'

In Nigeria there is a proverb that says, 'It is the heart that gives and the fingers just let go.' Giving is something only the heart can do and this is true not only of gift-giving but of all forms of giving. The heart knows that all belongs to all.

And so when we give from the heart, we are free. To give thanks means to give expression to mutual belonging. Genuine thanksgiving comes from the heart where we are rooted in universal belonging. Wholehearted thanksgiving engages the whole person. Even our sufferings and losses can become occasions of gratitude when we recognise through them the sufferings and losses of others, but also when we realise we are not abandoned, even if we abandon ourselves.

surprise
Wherever we may be, we are in some way engaged in universal give and take. If our feelings are too scarred and too jaded to fully vibrate to the great giving and receiving, we might at least find one small area in which we can spontaneously respond with joy.

Life is full of surprises, and surprise is the key to gratitude. Even if our life lacks the surprise of the extraordinary, the ordinary can always be surprising. The surprise of the unexpected wears off, but the surprise of freshness never wears off. In rainbows, it is obvious. Less obvious is the surprise of freshness present in the most ordinary things, but we can learn to see it as plainly as we see rainbows. Sometimes we have to train ourselves to spot it. Robert Frost calls it 'a mist from the breath of a wind/a tarnish that goes at the touch of a hand.'

One drop of surprise can lead to oceans of gratefulness. To recognise surprise is the beginning and the source of gratitude. In moments of surprise we catch a glimpse of the joy to which gratefulness opens the door. Even the predictable turns into a surprise the moment we stop taking it for granted. If we knew how the whole world worked, we could still be surprised that there was a universe at all, but if we don't think about it we won't be surprised at it. Our eyes are open to the surprise in the world around us the moment we wake up from taking things for granted.

Gratefulness is the measure of our aliveness. If we are numb, if we take things for granted, then we are dead, because to those who are awake to life's surprises, death lies behind, not ahead. To live life open to surprise, in spite of all that's dying around us, makes us even more alive.

Gratitude keeps us youthful. By being more and more grateful, we get younger every day. Surprise is the starting point. It opens our inner eye, because the amazing fact is that everything is a gift. Nothing can be taken for granted. If it can't be taken for granted, then we must be grateful. And as we begin to be grateful for small things, that gratitude grows and grows like expanding ripples on the surface on the pool.

A TIME TO FORGIVE

'Forgiveness goes beyond human fairness. It is pardoning those things that can't readily be pardoned at all.'

C S LEWIS

Forgiveness involves more than excusing. When we excuse somebody, we brush their mistake aside and do not punish them for it. When we forgive, we not only pardon a failing or a deliberate act of evil, but we also embrace the person responsible and seek to rehabilitate and restore them.

Our forgiveness may not always be accepted, but once we have reached out our hand we cleanse ourselves of resentment. We may remain deeply wounded, but we will not use our hurt to inflict further pain on another.

When we revisit a negative memory and chalk up another person's wrongs, we are creating a grudge. It doesn't matter if the cause of the grudge is real or imagined, the effect is the same. Once there, it will slowly eat away at us until it spills out and corrodes everything around us.

We all know bitter people. They have an amazing memory for the tiniest detail, and they wallow in self-pity and resentment. They catalogue every offence against them and are always ready to show others how much they have been hurt. On the outside they may appear to be calm and composed, but inside they are bursting with pent-up hatred.

These people defend their indignation constantly; they feel that they have been hurt too deeply and too often, and that somehow this exempts them from the need to forgive. But it is these very people who need to forgive most of all. Their hearts are sometimes so full of rancour that they no longer have the capacity to love.

Bitterness is more than just a negative outlook on life. It is destructive. Wilfully holding on to grudges against another person has a disastrous effect on the soul. It opens the door to evil and leaves us vulnerable to thoughts of spite, hatred and even violence. It destroys our souls, and it can destroy our bodies as well.

I recall a few years ago talking to a woman whose husband had died. She was an honest, capable, hard-working and dependable woman, yet she could not grieve or show any emotion and, after weeks of talk and struggle, the cause of her coldness became clear. She was unable to forgive her husband's faults, she could not point to one large hurt, but she was bowed down by hundreds of grudges. It was a salutary lesson.

forgiveness liberates us

Our freedom as human beings is grounded in forgiveness, for each of us repeatedly offends and is offended. Each of us is oppressor and oppressed, wounder and wounded.

Without forgiveness we are cemented into fixed roles, we cannot free ourselves from them. Forgiveness liberates us; forgiveness transforms us. The experience of forgiveness enables us to understand and accept our failures. We are released to carry on as responsible members of the human community.

Repentance and forgiveness do not mean the removal of our natural reactions, humiliations – anger, deep hurt, suspicion, mistrust – rather they introduce a new patience, a new understanding, a new degree of tolerance, all of which are precious. After we pay the price, a mysterious and miraculous peace creeps in where hostility used to dwell and the human spirit grows in wisdom and maturity.

Forgiveness is a daily challenge; the challenge to let go of our desire to control life and our need to direct outcomes and plan our own movements and of those around us. Forgiveness allows us to let go some of our expectations of others.

Forgiveness is a daily task. If we cannot live at peace amidst the problems and inadequacies of our daily surroundings, we're not likely to be ready to make peace with the more significant wounds and traumas of our life. These daily disturbances and challenges provide us with the opportunity to prepare for bigger moments of life and for the more demanding forgivenesses.

A forgiving attitude cannot develop as long as certain other attitudes persist. As long as we cling to our self-righteousness and sit in judgement on others, we cannot forgive. Forgiveness is power. It frees us from our past, overcoming every evil. It can heal both the person who is forgiving and the person forgiven. Forgiveness would change our whole world if we allowed it to flow through us unchecked. Too often we cannot do that, we stand in its way, not daring to unleash its power. We hold the keys of forgiveness in our own hands and we must choose each day whether or not to use them. Forgiveness is the way to peace and happiness. It is also a mystery and unless we seek it, it will remain hidden from us.

An act of forgiveness is the key to the defeat of evil. This is true in our own small worlds and in the wider world as well. As more hurt is inflicted, hostilities and resentment will grow. We create an unending cycle of pain to pain, aggression to acts of revenge. We can see this when quarrels and arguments begin, names are called, feelings of tension and division occur. Each one considers his or her integrity to be challenged, no-one will yield, no-one will say 'I did

NOW IS THE TIME

cheat'. No one says 'I'm sorry this occurred and let's make peace'.
And so it can go on indefinitely. World powers illustrate the same
sort of cycle. Too often we believe that forgiveness and reconciliation
are signs of weakness. The idea is to be tough, to stand up for
ourselves – not to give in and not to let anyone take advantage of us.

breaking the cycle

In 1960 Dag Hammarskjöld wrote, 'Forgiveness breaks the chain of
causes.' Without forgiveness we will remain prisoners of the vicious
circle between violence and injustice. Just as resentment is cyclical,
forgiveness is cyclical too. We cannot underestimate the miracle and
mystery of forgiveness. Gordon Wilson's forgiveness of the terrorists
whose bomb caused his daughter's death allowed him to come to
terms with his loss and its effect reached far beyond his own person.
He held his daughter's hand as they lay trapped beneath a mountain
of rubble. It was 1987 and he and Marie had been attending a
peaceful memorial service in Enniskillen, Northern Ireland, when the
bomb went off. Amazingly, Gordon refused to retaliate, saying that
angry words could neither restore his daughter nor bring peace to his
country.

Only hours after the bombing, he told the BBC reporters, 'I have
lost my daughter and we shall miss her, but I bear no ill will, I bear
no grudge, that will not bring her back. Don't ask me please for a
purpose, I don't have an answer, but I know that there has to be a
plan. If I didn't think that I would commit suicide. It's part of a
greater plan and we shall all meet again.' Later Gordon said that his
words were not intended as a logical response to his daughter's
murder. He had simply blurted them out from the depth of his heart.
In the days and months after the bombing, he struggled to live up to
his words. It wasn't easy, but they were something to hang on to,
something to keep him afloat in the dark hours.

There can be no forgiveness of others unless we believe we are
part of a common humanity. In practical terms this means believing
that no one individual, no one group, is superior to another. We may

be different in race and culture and religion and capacity, but we're all the same and each of us harbours a vulnerable heart.

To forgive means to believe that each of us can evolve and change, that human redemption is possible. We often lock people up in ready-made judgements. She is 'no good', he is 'lazy', etc. But they are much more than that, they are people who have loved, hoped, trusted, who can in some small way recognise their faults and their brokenness and can grow in humanity and inner freedom and in love.

To forgive means to begin to build unity and peace. Unity is the ultimate treasure, it is a place where each of us can grow, bear fruit, and give life, this is what we all yearn for. When someone loves deeply, forgiveness is evident. If we love and want all people to be free to bear fruit, we will be a people of forgiveness. We will no longer be governed by inner hurts or need to prove our worth.

It is not easy either to accept forgiveness or to forgive. It is not easy to shed our self-centredness. It is not easy to let go of our feelings of fear that prevent us from forgiveness and forgiving. At the heart of the process of forgiveness is a desire to be liberated from negative passions, sharp dislikes and hatred. This is the desire that starts us on the road to true forgiveness.

The love of one's enemy is at the heart of the Christian message. When Peter asked Jesus how many times should he forgive, 'Is it seven times?' 'No, seventy-times seven,' Jesus answered, which meant many, many, many times. Jesus said forcibly:

> *Love your enemies, do good to those who hate you. Speak well of those who speak badly of you, pray for those who abuse you.*

> LUKE 6:27–28

Throughout his life, Jesus frequently emphasised that we must forgive one another. Even in his answer to the disciples' request for a method of prayer, he included the need for forgiveness in a proactive way, 'And forgive us our trespasses as we forgive them.' He himself had forgiven many their debts and sins. Shortly before he died, he said, 'Father forgive them for they do not know what they are doing.' Jesus knew the transformative and liberating power of forgiveness.

The Dalai Lama also points out the same truth in Buddhism when he says:

> *The bodhisattva affirms the importance of acquiring the right attitude towards your enemy. If you know how to develop your attitude, your enemies become your spiritual masters because their presence gives you an opportunity to grow in tolerance, patience and understanding.*

In the Koran, forgiveness of enemies is also important:

> *It may be that Allah may grant love and friendship between you and those whom you now hold as enemies, for Allah has power over all things and Allah is oft forgiving and most merciful.*

Martin Luther King believed forgiveness had the potential to turn an enemy into a friend. He saw love and forgiveness as a part of his Christian faith, but he also knew the pragmatic way in which forgiveness worked. He knew that he and his fellow African-Americans would have to live, for decades to come, in the same areas in which they were campaigning for recognition of their civil rights. If they let themselves become bitter about their treatment, it would spill over into violence and that would simply lead to more bitterness and resentment in the future. Rather than breaking down the walls of racial hatred, it would build them up higher. He knew that only forgiving their oppressors would deliver African-Americans and white Americans from the descending spiral of destruction. Only forgiveness could point the way forward to a brighter future according to Martin Luther King.

> *We never get rid of an enemy by meeting hate with hate. We get rid of an enemy by getting rid of enmity. By its very nature, hate destroys and tears down. By its nature, love creates and builds. Love transforms with redemptive power.*

To forgive involves letting go of a feeling of resentment and of the vision that underlies that feeling, the vision in which we see ourselves as being offended against, the vision of self as a victim. The main spiritual shift that takes place in the event of being forgiven or forgiving is a new experiencing of self; blaming others falls away and we begin to accept primary responsibility for who we are.

forgiveness is a blessing

There are several common misunderstandings with regard to forgiveness. Forgiveness is some kind of foolish naivety that polishes over every wrong and explains evil away so that there is nothing left to forgive anymore. We cannot escape this difficult task so easily; forgiveness is much more serious than that. Nor is forgiveness a form of suppression that seeks peace at any price, avoiding confrontation with injustice. Suppression can never serve as a lasting solution to a problem. To vent one's anger may cause conflict and hostility, but suppressing one's anger has a price tag too. It leads to fatigue and depression. Anger is poison both in its uncontrolled expression and in its suppression. Forgiveness faces evil squarely and deals with it courageously and wisely. By forgiving we do not forget, but we remember differently. We remember in a manner that no longer harbours either resentment or bitterness and which no longer chains us to those who have done evil to us. Any great injustice that we have suffered remains stored in our memory, in our psyche, and sometimes in our bodies. The injury leaves scars that remind us of what has been done to us.

Forgiveness opens a path to the future, whereas resentment holds us captive. Forgiveness is not a kind of weakness that does not dare to face reality without conviction or genuine engagement. On the contrary, forgiveness is courageous and demands strength. Nor does forgiveness confer impunity. Even if the perpetrator has already been punished by the law or in some other just fashion, the victim will have to forgive. The law deals with the outside only. While it punishes the offender it does not free the victim. Forgiveness takes place in our very own hearts. On the other hand, forgiving a person his or her malice does not necessarily mean forgoing just punishment under the law.

Reconciliation requires two persons at least, while forgiveness can be achieved without any contact with the perpetrator. There can be times when forgiveness without any attempt at reconciliation is to be preferred, for instance in the case of rape. Forgiveness can be very difficult because something in our nature wants to keep holding on to our injury. Our justifiable resentment is like a precious possession. We can withdraw into our injured state and wallow in it, nurturing our resentment and pain. When we hold on to resentment, eventually something will die in us. Our humour, our spontaneity, our energy, our sense of self-worth. Resentment can also affect our health. Genuine forgiveness relieves us of this sinister and destructive baggage.

Forgiveness leads to greater maturity; starting out as passive victims without any control over our feelings, we end up acknowledging that we are the source of our emotions. Forgiveness is the slowly growing insight that we are not in control of other people. Thus forgiveness that is genuine is a great challenge. If we fail we will fall short in the development of our personality, of our life and in our relationship with God. We will end up in a circle of never-ending repetitions that could become neurotic. It is not until we truly forgive that something truly new will enter our lives where life will be able to develop freely again.

Resisting forgiveness saps our strength and wastes energy and joy. Forgiveness and forgiving are beyond the human; they occur in grace. Forgiveness cannot be accomplished on our own, it must be given to us. We are capable of forgiveness only if we are acted on by some reality outside of and beyond – and in some way greater than – ourselves. Forgivingness is a blessing, it is a gift and a grace to seek and to pray for.

A TIME TO HEAL

Hearts that have known pain meet in mutual recognition and trust.

RAM DASS / PAUL GORMAN

Healing is possible at all times. Indeed healing is a matter precisely of time. Healing takes time and time itself is a healer, which comes slowly, bringing acceptance and understanding in its wake. If we want to honour the fact that there is a time to heal, then we have to come to peace with the notion that healing does not come before its time, but happens with infinite slowness, in its own good time.

Healing comes mysteriously, we never quite know from where. Men and women of prayer, hidden away in monasteries and hermitages, bring healing in unknown ways to a world that is hurting, like hidden pumps irrigating dry lands.

Healing is full of respect. It is not seductive; it is a listening and a touch that awakens energies in the heart and body of the other. It communicates life and freedom; it gives a desire for life. Healing is a mother who, feeding her little child, reveals to her that she is

NOW IS THE TIME

beautiful. It is the nurse that touches and tends the wounds with reverence and care so as to cause the patient as little pain as possible. There is healing also in professionalism, competence, efficiency. It is when all of these come together, tenderness, gentleness, communication, efficiency professionalism, that true healing takes place.

ancient cultures

Ancient cultures often had methods of healing that are very different from our modern scientific approach to medicine. One such culture that survives today is that of the aboriginal peoples of Australia. *The Mutant Message* by Marlo Morgan tells of the incredible healthcare talents of an aboriginal tribe who have never studied biochemistry or pathology, but who have a commitment to wellness. 'What appeared miraculous from my point of view,' the writer says, 'was obviously the norm in tribal perspective.' This tribe believes that what is happening in the mind and heart of the person being healed and of the healer is more important than the actions of the healer. These healers work by sending thoughts of perfection to the body; there is as much going on in their heads and hearts as in their hands. According to their beliefs, if the patient and healer are open and receptive to receiving wellness and believe in a state of full and complete recovery, it happens. They believe that we are not random victims of ill health, that the physical body is the only means our internal conscious has to communicate with our consciousness.

We westerners have developed the most sophisticated healthcare techniques, yet we do not seem able to listen to ancient healing practices that have been saving lives for centuries. If we are prepared to try their methods at all, we do so only with great caution and on a selected few conditions. In the meantime people live and die unhealed and the physician tells the family that everything within his or her power has been done.

Of course, all pain, maybe even most pain, is not physical, though there is often a relationship between physical illness and pain and emotional or spiritual pain. Slowing down the body allows us to look around us and to analyse the really important wounds that we need to mend, wounded relationships, gaping holes in our belief system, walled-up tumours of fear, eroding faith, hardened emotions, unforgiveness.

nature heals

I live with some other members of my community in a small house in the heart of the city. It is in a built-up area, but we have a small 'sanctuary garden' that we are just developing from bare soil into what we plan as a place of rest and restoration, where people can sit and relax or meditate in the sunshine or the shade, a sacred space for healing the spirit among the plants and flowers, an oasis of calm in the midst of the city.

I watch with amazement the development of that garden. Some of the seeds we sowed there are so tiny it is hard to believe that there is so much genetic information in them; some are such odd shapes that it is hard to believe they are seeds at all. It is such a delight, some weeks after the planting, to watch the seedlings begin to poke their way through the prepared soil, followed by the leaves that proclaim the plant's identity, and to watch as each plant becomes so specifically itself.

Preparing good soil for plants and then seeing them respond is healing work, as is just sitting still and watching and waiting, 'listening' to the seeds growing. For people who are sick in their bodies, as well as for those of us with inner afflictions, being able to work in a garden can be extraordinarily healing. It is a healing experience to see the fruits of our labour appear instead of always being the one who is laboured over. To start to take care of the garden instead of needing to be cared for all the time can be the beginning of healing for the sick.

pain

According to the nineteenth-century English essayist Charles Lamb, 'Pain is life; the sharper the pain the more evidence of life.' We all experience pain of some sort in our lives, whether it is physical pain and illness or psychological or spiritual damage, but such is our fear of pain that we sometimes try to cope with it by denying it. We are afraid to acknowledge our pain, hoping that by denying it we can control it. One reason we persist in this strategy is that it works, up to a point. If we are successful in our denial of our pain, we can have the illusion that it is under control. But that is not healing: that is merely temporary containment.

Another reason that we deny our pain is that we are afraid of appearing to be losers. We live in a culture that is committed to achievement and success, and so we move faster every day, maybe not even noticing that we are hurting as we compete in the race to success and security. And all the time we pretend that we are fine, that nothing is wrong.

Healing comes when we acknowledge and yet move beyond the hurt. If the first step towards healing is acknowledging that we are in pain, the next step is being prepared to let go of our pain. To be healed we have to want to be healed. To be healed we must move beyond our pain, outside of it, in spite of it. Healing depends on our wanting to be well. We may not forget what we have suffered, but we must choose not to let it control us or imprison us, because we know that there is more to life than that.

healing ourselves and others

Oscar Wilde once wrote: 'Where there is sorrow there is holy ground.' We are all capable both of being healers and of being healed, but unless we are open to our own woundedness and our own need to be healed, then we will not be open to the woundedness of others, and so we cannot act as healers. We can only bring compassion to others if we have experienced it ourselves.

If we are open, then as we bind the emotional wounds of others, we find new meaning in life, a new love for the unknown other and the unknown self, and we will be able to give and receive as we are healing and being healed. When we reach out to others in their pain as they touch in to ours, a new life is opened to us.

Whenever healing takes place, there is always more than one being healed and always more than one needing to be healed. By taking those whom they are healing into their arms and into their hearts, healers learn from those they are healing about human conditions they themselves would never have understood without the wounded. We all need healers who listen and understand us and who heal us with their healing powers and with their compassion, but we also need the wounded and hurt who speak to us about their hurt and who touch into our own hurt and woundedness. Reaching out to the other doesn't stop there. There is also a reaching back into ourselves, there is a reaching from the other to the next and so it goes on and on and on. Healing never begins or ends with one person, healing goes on and on and on and it occurs on all levels of our being, physical, emotional, mental and spiritual.

our enemies as healers

Our enemies may be our greatest healers, but only if we are open to them. Our enemies are people who challenge us. They are people with whom we do not agree, who block us, who contradict us, who stifle us, people who are not for us. Their presence seems to bring out in us envy and jealousy and either aggression or a sort of regression. We see them as everything we are not ourselves and their presence reminds us that we are not that. Or they ask too much of us and we cannot respond to their demands, so we push them away. We believe that our enemies endanger us. We dislike them; we might even wish that they didn't exist. Because our enemies frighten us, we are unable to hear what they are asking of us. We allow them, in one way or another, to dominate us, to stifle us. We often run away and we may wish they would run away too.

We have our personal enemies, and then there are people we see as enemies of society in general. The most despised people in our society are probably money-lenders, who line their pockets on the misery of those who are already miserable, and drug-pushers, who likewise exploit the misery of the weakest in our society and make money from their despair. The equivalent in the time of Jesus would have been the tax-collectors, who not only collected taxes on behalf of the Roman invaders, but did so in unscrupulous ways and lined their own pockets at the expense of the poor. We despise people like this, we condemn them, we reject them, we want to have nothing to do with them, and yet it is precisely this sort of person that Jesus called out to, because he saw into the heart of the tax-collector and he saw goodness there. This is how Jesus told his followers to behave:

> *I say to you: love your enemies, do good to those who hate you, bless those who curse you, pray for those who treat you badly. To the one who slaps you on the cheek, present the other cheek too.*

> LUKE, 6:27

This is the ultimate, at times seemingly impossible, challenge of the New Testament and the Christian way of life. But the point is that the faults that we see in our enemies are often the ones that we refuse to face in ourselves. The very people that we despise are people who in some way or another remind us of those parts of ourselves that still need to be healed. There is no evil in this world that we are not capable of committing. If we look into our heart we will find what we are afraid of, if we make a list of the people we don't like or things we don't like to see happening, the kinds of actions that we despise and that we condemn, we will discover that these are the parts of ourselves that are not yet healed, that we disown, that we are ashamed of. Seeing these places in ourselves, we fear that maybe some day the evil in ourselves might come to light, so we project it onto other people and that makes us feel better and we are self-righteous in denouncing them.

It also happens in society, when we rejoice to see prisoners behind bars because we like to believe that we are better than they are. We see it again when there is great delight in exposing the scandals of public figures, instead of discovering what is going on in our own hearts and accepting that there is much in us that needs to be healed, and even as we heal one part of ourselves, we will discover more and more layers of us that need healing. Healing is the work of a lifetime.

If we can face our enemies as Jesus recommended, then we can face ourselves more honestly and we can be healed, because our enemies challenge us to free ourselves from old habits or blind spots and develop in full the potential of our beauty and our sensitivities as human beings. It is there exactly, in our relationship to our enemies, that the healing process can take place, because what our enemies do is highlight for us our own weakness and our lack of maturity, our inner poverty, the poverty that makes it difficult for us to look at them.

We all struggle to hold onto the old ways of doing things, but there is always an alternative. We can learn to use the difficulties we have with our relationships; if we can accept our enemies as opportunities to waken and bring forth new qualities of healing in us, we can open our hearts and allow the finest human qualities – awareness, compassion, humour, wisdom and a fearless dedication to truth – to grow and develop. If we choose this approach, even the most difficult relationships become a pathway of deep connection with ourselves and with others, not just with those we know and love easily, but those we have had difficulty in loving. All this will heal and expand our hearts.

Reaching out to our enemies challenges us because it costs us what we hold dear, namely our old ways of staying secure and defended; but it is exactly in this situation that the opportunity to be open arises; if we open up in this way our relationships will deepen immeasurably and we will become more flexible and responsive to life as a whole.

And in that meeting with our enemy who challenges, we are not only healed ourselves, but we can actually bring healing to the enemy, because they experience in us a love that they have never experienced before – because we see their lovableness. We see the good qualities that they may not know that they have or which they may never have seen in themselves and we see their positive potential, we see the heart of a child within them which we have never seen before and which they may never have seen before, because they may never have met a loving, gentle, compassionate, caring person expressing a healing, compassionate love.

heartbreak heals

When we feel the pain of the constriction between the perfect love in our hearts and the obstacles to its complete realisation, it breaks our heart. When the heart breaks open we hurt, and in this pain we feel raw and tender, but we are at that point in touch with the very core of who we are. The heart can never really break, for it is already by nature soft and receptive. When our heart breaks, what really breaks is the defensive shell around the heart, which we have constructed to try to protect our soft spot, where we feel most deeply affected by life. When that is exposed, we feel a presence of reality that we never did before. When our heart breaks out of the protective shell, we shed our ideal images of how we should be and we feel naked and it is in this nakedness that we taste the essential nature of our existence and we are healed.

tenderness

Healing is always tender, but tenderness does not mean sentimentality and a show of emotion. Rather it is unearthing gentleness and kindness, which shows another person that we consider them important and precious. Tenderness is revealed through gesture and tone of voice. It is not weakness, but a reassuring strength, transmitted through the eyes and the body. It is revealed in the attitude of the one, completely attentive to the other. It does not impose itself; it is not aggressive; it is gentle and humble. It does not issue orders.

Much of our capacity to heal another depends on our state of mind. Being able to listen is one of the greatest gifts that we can offer one another. To listen and hear, we have to be aware of the chattering that goes on in our minds, judging thinking, evaluating, leaping in, taking things personally, being bored, being distracted, reacting – these are all part of everybody's life. Sometimes we are so scattered that we are not even aware that we are not present, that we are using our minds to try and solve some other problem, that we are only half listening.

meditation and awareness

There is a pull in all of us to fix things, to look for solutions. The mind tries to do too many things at once and in our attempts to heal we may increase the distance between ourselves and the person we are with. So it is that there is less room to meet the other, less room for relationships to emerge, less room for healing. This kind of agitation isn't a surprise for most of us; most of us come to expect and accept it.

Yet it need not be so. Because of our mind's capacity to think, we tend to believe that thinking is the only attribute that our minds have. Being aware is the deepest capacity and quality of our minds. We can develop a deep conscious awareness if we are willing to acknowledge the agitation of our minds. And there are many ways in which this can happen.

The practice of meditation is one way of accessing our deeper qualities of mind and in that way we can deepen our powers to heal. These deeper qualities and inner calm, sharper concentration, deep intuitiveness, understanding and an ability to tune into the other is a very important part of healing. In healing, our awareness remains quiet and clear, with breadth and perspective, it is broad and deep and yet it is also focused; with all of this we are not only thinking participants but observers of our thinking and our participation as well. Healing then becomes an act of reverence and everything becomes important – the smallest act, the way we fill a glass of water and hand it to somebody, the way we comfort a child, the way we listen to a person's story – these are part of a healing process that goes on way beyond us.

memory as healing

There is a healing in remembering or re-membering, putting back together the members or parts of a thing, putting things together. Mystics can teach us to remember by modelling for us an attitude of inwardness and mindfulness, a capacity to be open-eyed and open-hearted.

Memory enables us to recall our blessings, to give thanks for them to grow because of them. Good memories encourage us, warm us and help us to keep hope in our hearts. They serve us as a way of keeping us connected with our past. Good memories can strengthen us and sustain us. Nancy Wood writes, 'Going from this place to another place is like a bird in winter. She remembers the beauty of her springtime nest just to keep herself from freezing.'

The ability to remember is a precious gift that fills our hearts with gratitude. The German philosopher of the early twentieth century, Heidegger, sees ours as a culture of forgetfulness; we easily lose the power of remembering. But we need to hold on to our memories, because without memory we would be unable to savour the good things that have happened to us in the past or cherish the things that are happening to us now.

Not all our memories are good, of course, and some memories can haunt us, depending on what they stir in us, and how we receive and live with them. But even our unpleasant memories can be a source of healing, because they may be calling for attention, they may be prompting us about things in our past, painful things, that need to be dealt with so that then we can move on and focus on the memories that can strengthen us.

It is important to catch the memories that enhance our goodness and draw forth the goodness in us; to catch them, to dwell on them, to savour them. In these we will find hope and inspiration for the future. To be able to remember requires silence, and in the silence of our hearts there is an inexhaustible richness, there is a great healing store of the past, in comparison with the fullness of which all the present is merely a trickle.

A TIME TO COME HOME

*In order to possess what you do not possess, you must go by the way
of dispossession.*

T S ELIOT

Home is a place in which to feel safe and secure, warm and dry and
protected. A place to rest and eat, sleep and be entertained, find
solitude and pray, love and laugh, argue and cry, read a book, share a
meal, watch a television programme, play an instrument, do a bit of
gardening, play with the children, have a drink, get the housework
done and the bills paid, be at ease with oneself and with friends and
family, in safety and security, without fear of interference or
intrusion.

The need for a place like that is deep and urgent in all of us. The
desire for a place to call home is the deepest need in every human heart
and perhaps the least recognised. And yet for many people, home is
elusive, unattainable, beyond their grasp, because something has
happened in their lives, some catastrophic event has separated them
from home and they can find it almost impossible to come home
again, to secure a place of their own where they are safe and at ease.

homelessness

People who find themselves homeless are people who are going through a transition in their lives. Perhaps they are moving from one home to another and have somehow got stranded in between; perhaps they are in transition from the family home to adult independence, and something has gone wrong for them; perhaps they have been mentally ill and they are in transition to healing but they haven't yet found their new place in the community; perhaps they are fleeing from violence or abuse and are trying to find a place where they can be safe and protected.

The danger is that people in transition can sometimes get trapped in the transitional phase of their lives and never make it to the other side, to the place they set out for. What began as a stage in their lives, an unfortunate occurrence where they managed to slip through the net of provision for people at risk, can quickly develop into a state of life, a way of being in the world, homeless, friendless, isolated, marginalised, insecure. If there is nobody to give them a helping hand at this crucial transitional stage in their lives, they can easily slip into a whole way of life that is without hope; those who are weak can get destroyed, those who are mentally insecure can slip into insanity, those who are young can easily get sucked into a life of crime and violence, those who are sexually vulnerable can be exploited and end up living a life of prostitution and degradation.

Homeless people have no possessions and they have no security. Before long they have no self-respect either, and if they are not helped to come home, they may end up becoming bitter and resentful, maybe even destructive towards themselves and towards others. All of them have something infinitely beautiful in their hearts, they may be a good bit troubled, but they can be made whole again if someone looks, notices, pays attention to them, helps them.

I've known homeless people who are maybe only just a little bit perplexed, frightened and intimidated; people who are maybe reading things a little differently from the way they are meant to be read; people who are still living, walking in the same world as we do, except that they walk just a little obliquely; people perhaps who aren't at home in cities and lose themselves in them, as in a wood or a forest that has no ending.

These homeless ones are people who are familiar with pain every day, who live in dreadful fear of being beaten up, of being abused, brutalised, robbed, even killed. Some may express this fear by lashing out against society, because it is their only way to protect themselves. Or maybe they can no longer stand the noise of the city and they cover their heads and block their ears and shut themselves in on themselves. Some are children who are left on the streets, open to all kinds of exploitation – prostitution, drugs, crime, drink – and to defend themselves, they have to hide their feelings, block them off and cut them out, live on the edge of society and of themselves as they make their way through the streets quickly, or sit for a long time in gardens and open spaces and bus stations and doorways, their heads sunk into their hands.

not just shelter
Sometimes, the need for a home is confused with the physical need simply for shelter. If you ask people to describe home, they will usually begin by describing a house or a flat – places, in other words, of shelter. Certainly home must have a physical embodiment – it has to be a place, and it has to provide shelter – but equally certainly the physical framework by itself does not constitute a home. One reason we tend to confuse shelter with home is that when we see people on the streets whom we recognise as homeless, what we see is people who are without shelter, who literally have no place, other than the pavement, to lay their head.

Shelter may be the first constituent of a home but it is not the only one. It is not enough to give a person shelter and a bed for the night in order to deal with their homelessness; giving them a bed that they can count on again the next night and the next night is a step in the right direction, but it is still not enough, that is still providing not a home, but shelter only. People need shelter, but they also need security, love, warmth and above all to belong – in short they need a place to call home.

There is a moment in *Nicholas Nickleby* by Charles Dickens that illustrates what I mean very well. Nicholas had befriended a young crippled boy named Smike while he was working in a children's home. When Smike discovered that Nicholas was leaving the home, he wanted to go with him, but Nicholas was poor and was unable to offer Smike a proper home. Smike, however, was not thinking of practical matters, like food, clothes or shelter; instead he turns to Nicholas and says with passion, 'You are my home.' The home that Smike seeks in Nicholas is not physical shelter but a loving presence where he feels safe. Home has little to do with walls and roofs that keep out the wind and the rain; the best home is a place in the heart where there is room for loving relationships.

Theodor Zeldin, an English historian and anthropologist, puts the distinction between shelter or housing and home like this: 'If home is… one of the great personal and collective works of art that all humans spend their lives attempting to raise up and keep from falling down, then the art of creating homes as distinct from building houses still has a long way to go, and still remains within the province of magic.'

displaced people

People who are out-of-home are displaced. They have lost their place in our world as it is organised with streets and houses and addresses, and they live in a sort of no-man's-land, a bleak territory with no houses and no addresses, just endless confusion, rejection and pain.

Sometimes a whole people or whole groups of people can get displaced, by war, as a result of natural disaster or because of persecution or economic necessity. As a people, we in Ireland have had a long history of displacement, emigration, diaspora. Now we in our turn, like most countries in the prosperous West, are experiencing a small but steady influx of refugees, asylum seekers and economic immigrants, people who have lost not only their homes but their homeland, and very often their families, their culture, their pride and their hope.

As you enter America from Europe you pass the Statue of Liberty, and on that statue is inscribed a verse by Emma Lazarus: 'Send these the homeless, tempest-tossed to me, I will lift my lamp beside the golden door.' But there is hardly a country in the world today that can claim to welcome the tempest-tossed with open arms. There is very little welcome here in Ireland for those who come from the 'wrong' part of the world. We tend to view them as competitors for scarce jobs and liabilities in our welfare and social-services systems, and so people who have experienced hatred in their own country are subjected to it again in their new country.

Our immigrants and asylum seekers are just another, particularly visible set of displaced people in our midst. They can stand, in a way, if we are prepared to face their pain and look them in the eye, for all those we displace and reject, perhaps more unobtrusively, such as our own homeless people; our addicts; our Travellers; the people we have hidden away in mental hospitals, prisons, emergency shelters; people living with AIDS; all who are ostracised and displaced and considered society's undesirables and unwanted people.

inner homelessness
Most people reading this are likely to have a home, a place to be at peace and at rest. Nevertheless, we can all identify with being out-of-home. We have all experienced times when we are not at home within ourselves, when we have felt that we are wasting our spiritual inheritance, when we have lost touch with the inner resources of our being, when our inner soul is in a lonely wasteland. To be out of home in our heart at this level is to be a stranger to love. There are some people who have never known love. Such people have never been at home with themselves; they have never had the sense of being precious in God's hands; they have never realised that God has called them by their name and loved them.

We are all homeless in our heart when we feel rejected, when we feel we are not known and not loved, not precious, when our image of ourselves is poor. These are areas that we try to block out from ourselves and others; we try not to see or taste or touch our unloveliness. There is something within every human spirit that does not relish that land of homelessness, yet too much companionship and security covers over the rawness of reality and prevents us from encountering the mystery of our inner homelessness. Our homelessness is a secret territory in which we can discover our true selves.

We have all had moments of desolation, when we have been full of opposition to everything, when everything that gives joy to other people seems to delude and deceive us. When we pay attention to homeless people, we will see people like ourselves who are trying to form sentences, who are trying to find a way of coping with the madding crowd, with the terrible noise, with the stress of insecurity. The homeless person can awaken in us awareness of our own homelessness, our own brokenness, our own need for silence, our poverty, when the silence of the night tells us about our human condition. In each homeless person we can find parts of ourselves – a childhood that has been lost, for example.

Partly because we can see ourselves in them, we often feel threatened by homeless people. They can evoke in us a fear that we might become like them, remembering the times when we too were ignored and powerless, when somebody passed us by without noticing us, or when someone dismissed us with a cursory judgement or a disparaging glance.

We can allow our fear of our own homelessness to cause us to reject homeless people, to distance ourselves from them, to put them in a category that is different from the category where we put ourselves. Or we can listen to what it is that homeless people have to teach us about ourselves.

After spending nearly twenty years living and working with the social services in Kilkenny, I came, with a heavy heart, to live in

Dublin in the early 1980s. I did not feel at home in Dublin and I missed my work and my friends in Kilkenny. But very soon I was drawn into a study of homeless women in Dublin, which turned out to be a turning point in my life. That study and that first group of homeless women that I met led me into a whole new area of work, the area in which I have spent my life since then, working with and for and on behalf of people who have no homes, in Dublin and around the country. These men and women, young people and children have taught me many things and gifted me in many ways, but their greatest gift to me was to reveal to me my own homelessness, my own poverty, my own human fragility and my deep desire to be at home with myself, with other people and with God.

our true home

Homelessness of the soul reveals to us something of the darkness of human existence. It is an experience we all shy away from, but it can help us to realise our need for something greater than ourselves. We sit on a small planet and are able to count only a few stars. Being aware of this brings home to us our exile. Our physical homes and our human loves comfort us and may make us hide from or even deny the larger reality.

The larger reality is the divine. It is in that larger reality, in that mystery, in that sense of something that is beyond us that we can discover that our true home is not this earth but elsewhere. In our homelessness of the soul, we can hear the voice of God inviting us 'to make your home in me', and it is that invitation, that promise and hope that makes our homelessness tolerable. We can endure it because we know that ultimately we have a home, a home that will be revealed to us; but in order to reach that ultimate home, we need first to realise, to recognise and to experience our spiritual homelessness and to acknowledge and embrace it.

We all need to come home. We need to have a place that we can call home and we need to belong to a society and a culture. We need to be at home within our own hearts; we need to find a home in the hearts of others; and we need to be at home with our God. The journey home for all of us is different, longer or shorter, physically, socially, emotionally, spiritually. Our whole life is that journey home, the journey from home to home and threshold to threshold.

A TIME FOR A LITTLE LIGHT

My grandfather was a fisherman. He fished off the Kerry coast. My mother used to tell me how her mother worried about him when he went out to sea at the dead of night, in a tiny, fragile boat. There was no lighthouse on the coast where my grandfather fished, but the fishermen had their own ways of avoiding dangers, their own watches in the night. The light that guided them home they called the *leaca ré*, meaning the moon hill-slope. The slope of the hill was Slea Head, and the light of the moon and stars shone on the smooth stones on this slope and guided them home. The *leaca ré* was their lighthouse: the reflection in the moonlight was the beacon light that led them home out of the dark of the sea.

lighthouses

We all need a *leaca ré* in our lives, a beacon to help us find and drop anchor in our true home within ourselves. We need people who will act like lighthouses and show us the way, people who will light our journey for us. People who throw light for us are people who help us to become more aware, more attentive, so that we can see things as they are; people who tell us to slow down, take another route; people who will be there for us when the going is rough and choppy.

We tend to think in abstractions much of the time, and this tendency to make the concrete abstract distances us from the realities of life and makes it difficult at times to distinguish between truth and falsity. We need people who can help us to make the abstract concrete; who will turn percentages and statistics into people for us; who will unmask our false idols; who can help us to interpret what we hear through the media; who will throw the light of human values on public issues; who can combine prophecy and protest, no matter how difficult it is; who will show us the apartheid that exists in every society, including our own.

We need people who will enlighten us so that we learn to see how intimately we are connected with the world we live in and that we cannot live our lives as tourists, shirking our responsibility, indifferent to the effects of what we do on people in other parts of the world. People who enlighten us are people who can help us to understand our history and to assess society's agenda within the framework of humanity, creativity and spirituality. People who act as lighthouses for us can point out to us how we live in ignorance of the implications of our lifestyles and choices. The cheapest fruit, for example, that we can buy at our local supermarket may well be expensive for those who picked it in South Africa or Honduras, and we need to be aware of that and to make our decisions accordingly.

Religions can easily become private and personal systems, with no connection to the world. Most especially in our churches and among our spiritual leaders, we need people with the vision to piece together the dichotomy between the secular and the spiritual and close the distance between the private and the public. We need people who can convince us that there are no areas of human life that are not subject to moral and spiritual values and who will challenge us to live a more coherent, congruent and credible form of human community. We need people who can correct our limited understanding of what it is to be human.

sources of light

Traditionally, monks and mystics have been sources of light for humanity, but activists too can act as lighthouses in a dark world, shedding the light of their insight by their example and their work. Dorothy Day was such a lighthouse in her time. She worked with the homeless and the poor, crossing the borders of race and creed all over the United States and in other countries too. She wrote: 'If our cause is a mighty one and if we oppose the powers of darkness, we are working on the side of life. To stand on the side of life we must give up our own lives.' And that is what she did, giving her life to those she worked with.

Jean Vanier, founder of the L'Arche movement, which looks after people with mental disabilities in many parts of the world (including Ireland), is a shining light for us all, sharing with us through his writings and his work his profound insight into the dignity and value of even the most damaged human beings.

Another lighthouse was Simone Weil. From a well-to-do Jewish–French family herself, Weil had a strong senses of solidarity with working people and, though frail in health, she took on the life of a peasant, working in the vineyards and sending donations to political prisoners. She believed we should love one another in the same way as the sun loves us, gratuitously and universally. Unattached to any organised religion, she was at home on the borders between mathematics and Marxism, Judaism and Christianity, ancient philosophy and mysticism, the wealthy classes and the workers.

We can read about the work of people like Weil, Day and Vanier and be touched by them and enlightened by their vision, but it is not only the great thinkers and teachers who shed light on our world for us. People who are poor and marginalised, despite their poverty and even at times their despair, can also act as lighthouses for us. They challenge us to look at ourselves and the world we have created in a new way. They challenge us to look at our way of life, how much we waste, how much we want, how much we have or want that we don't need. They are like loudspeakers, shouting at us about our greed and our lack of generosity, but we are often deaf to their cries.

I know a woman in her forties who didn't have the opportunity for education in her youth, but who is now studying and preparing to go to university. Recently she told me that she had just won a competition for an essay on women and violence. She wrote about a woman who had lived a life of violence, basing her essay on a story someone told her in a bus many years earlier. She was able to pay attention to that woman's story to the extent that it was still vivid in her mind twenty years later. I admired the sensitivity to another person's problems and the attentiveness that this showed, but I was even more touched when she told me that she had decided to give half of the £30 she had won to a home for women who have been living with violence. This woman has an income herself of less than £60 a week.

We can all become sources of light for the people we live and work with, but if we want to do this, we need to learn to invest something of ourselves in everyone that we meet and to bring gifts of encouragement and hope wherever we go. In order to shed our light, we need to be patient with the darkness. We need to learn to trust and let go instead of clinging to our collected goods and to our illusions. If we are bored with life, paralysed with fear and guilt, we won't be able to shed light for those around us, but if we are open to exploring the creative potential of our families, workmates and companions, instead of being quick to criticise, we can become sources of light for them, encouraging them in their endeavours, leading them home.

If we are to become lights for others, we have to let go of the protected territory that we feel is ours, even though that goes against the grain and against our long-cultivated habits. Letting go doesn't come easy to any of us. For all of us there are objects and possessions, status and positions of distinction that block and blind us, and yet we hold on to them because we think we can't surrender them.

a personal experience

Seven years ago I became very ill, but I neglected my illness. I had difficulty in acknowledging my own frailty. Because of this, I got more and more ill, until I finally had to give in, because I was both physically very ill and psychologically worn out. At the time I was director of Focus Ireland (then called Focus Point), an organisation that works with homeless people and that I had established some years earlier. By this time it had become a big, thriving, growing organisation. At the same time, I was trying to help my family to care for my eighty-nine-year-old father.

I found it extremely difficult to accept that I had to stop, that I had to take rest, that I was not going to be the person who was in charge of everything. All my certainties and securities began to disappear. It was like entering a tunnel and not being quite sure if I would come out again. As I watched and waited in a state of not knowing I began to realise, as T S Eliot put it, that 'what you do not know is the only thing you know'. I did not know if I had a future; the past had been swept away, as it were; and I was in a waiting period. I felt that I was on the fringe, on the edge, afraid to look to the right or to the left, lest I fell into the dark abyss beneath and around me. I felt a sense of helplessness and powerlessness I had never known before. It was a dark, dark, Good Friday experience.

I was fortunate to have a good doctor and guide who never doubted my capacity to be well again. I was fortunate to have many supportive relatives, friends and colleagues, who waited, mostly in silence but at the same time giving me support, for me to get better. I was fortunate also to have a strong, determined will to be well that never faltered. But above all I was fortunate to have a deep faith and to know that even in my darkest, emptiest, most desolate moments that my God was always there. Even when I didn't *feel* this, I *knew* that this was so. Deep down in me I knew that there was some reason in all this misery and darkness.

It seemed to last for ever, but in fact it only lasted five or six weeks. Today I can say that that was one of the most important times in my life. It was a time for the old in me to die and the new to be born, the mighty to be fallen and the lowly to be lifted up. A way was opened in me to a new understanding and a new sensitivity and a new hope that made space for my own fragility and the fragility of the most forlorn and the most broken of human beings. It also helped me to realise how much more was hidden within me, how much more wisdom and beauty was still to be uncovered and discovered and brought into the light by way of the darkness.

As Eliot says, 'To arrive where you are, you must go by a way wherein there is no ecstasy.' I realised that I could never again take for granted the many things that I had taken for granted before. As I got well, I began to understand my own humanity, and in its own way, my illness gave me an inner light. It helped me to connect my frailty and brokenness with the brokenness of the world in a totally new way.

But it is not enough to see light and to recognise lights, however small and weak, as I did after my illness; we must also be willing to become lights ourselves, to extend ourselves, open ourselves to every experience, facing it squarely and letting it affect us. Being people of light and hope does not mean that we will not feel afraid; rather it means that we are willing to stay open to our fear and not run away. To wake up and confront what is actually happening rather than just going along with old stories and reactions and patterns is an act of hope, an act of faith, an action of great courage and an act of light.

discovering our own light

The great Indian philosopher and poet Tagore says, 'Only in the deepest silence of night the stars smile and whisper amongst themselves.' A lighthouse has no function in the day time; a beacon shines only when there is darkness. To discover the light that is within us, we must go through the darkness. When Christ said that he was the light of the world, he was not talking only about an external, prophetic light, but about an internal light that was the light at the heart of the universe and the light at the heart of every living person. When he called Christians to let their light shine before the world, he was talking about the light that shines from our innermost being, that part of us where God has written his name on us.

There is an oriental proverb that says, 'Pearls lie not on the seashore; if thou desirest one, thou must dive for it.' Similarly, to find our true light, the light that beckons and enlightens, we must go deep into ourselves, and the deeper we go, the brighter will be our light. It is then that we can be true lights to the world. We can't all be blazing lighthouses or glaring neon lights. Many of us are just flickering wicks that need to be pared and cared for, very gently, carefully and confidently. Still, even flickering lights can lead people to their true selves.

now is the time

No matter how oppressed we may be, we always retain some capacity to choose light over darkness. We can choose to risk ourselves to goodness or to give in to the power that oppresses us. The choice is totally up to us. When we take risks, when we let the props go and give ourselves up to the struggle, our gifts and potential are more radiant than at other times.

Being a person of light means being willing to move out and sit at the edge of our pain, our fear, our anger, our grief. It means taking our seat there on the edge and looking into our pain instead of being controlled by it. In essence, it is being willing to connect with our experience, to cultivate our ability to be in the present moment and to feel with our heart, even in situations that are difficult and painful. Being light means waiting without being afraid of the dark, of the silence and of the emptiness, for it is precisely in emptiness, darkness and nothingness that light is brought forth.

We can all shine our lights, if we are prepared to do it. Many people believe they cannot influence others, but they miss the point. The light will shine if the light is there, just as the sun effortlessly radiates its light when the time is right.

But it takes courage to be a light. It takes courage to disagree with government policies. It takes courage to stand up for marginalised people – homeless people, Travellers, Aborigines, Native-Americans – in the face of criticism. It takes courage to say, I believe that everybody has a right to a place to call home. It takes courage to say, I believe there are people in prisons who shouldn't be there, to say that we should be providing for them in the community in a new and different way. It takes courage to lay ourselves open to criticism if we differ from the mainstream and to be prepared to enter into discussion and debate. It is often easier to keep quiet, on the grounds that we gain nothing from upsetting people.

It takes courage to say certain things, and it takes courage to do certain things too. It takes courage to forgive our enemies and visit them in prison. It takes courage to refuse to work extra hours for money and to choose to give that time instead in voluntary service. It takes courage to refuse a rise in salary because we don't need it. It takes courage to leave an overpaid job for a lesser-paid one where the work is more worthwhile. It takes courage to refuse birthday or wedding or jubilee presents and ask instead that the money be give to a voluntary organisation working with people who are poor or homeless or otherwise marginalised, as a friend of mine did just recently. It takes courage, because we don't want to be unacceptable or to live on the fringes of society, as the poor do.

When we stick up for these principles, we may face criticism, rejection and even ridicule. It is not an effort to be taken lightly, because we can only face the world around us and say such things when we have first faced ourselves and know who we are and what we stand for. In other words, we must first have found the light within us.

Each of us has the capacity to be a light to the world, but to do that we must be prepared to let go of things; we must shrink to allow room for plurality and communion; we must allow our egos to be shattered. If we are to be lights, we must learn to give without calculating the loss and we must be willing to stand alone.

Now is our time. This is our time to make a difference, to be a light. This is our time to develop the best in ourselves so that we can make the best possible world for everyone.

A TIME FOR PEACE AND JUSTICE

Peace and justice are commonly considered to be quite different concepts; yet we can't have them separately. If we have justice, then peace flows from that; and without peace there is no justice. We can walk and march, write and speak, facilitate, lobby and advocate for justice, but if we cannot sit peacefully with ourselves, we will never be peace-filled people, we will never be givers of peace or bringers of justice, whatever else we may be.

I see justice and peace in terms of right relationships. If our relationship with our own self is right, then we are at peace with ourselves and in ourselves; and if our relationships with other people and with the world are right, then we have justice. But we can't have right relationships with others unless our relationship with our self is right – so we can't have justice without peace. And if our relationship with God is right also, then we have true peace with justice.

inner peace

To be people of peace and justice we must live in our own inner peace. Peace comes to us when we plumb our own depths, take the measure of ourselves and find the world within us. Peace comes when we have met and accepted the best and the worst within ourselves. Peace comes when we have faced our own questions, the questions only we can ask ourselves, which in the end are the only questions that matter.

Inner peace comes from knowledge of ourselves and acceptance of ourselves and from knowing that what is outside us can never destroy our true selves. When peace comes into our lives, a quietness sets in and there is nothing that anyone can do to us that can destroy or upset our equilibrium.

Inner peace makes us wise. When we know what goes on in our own heart we have more respect for the struggles of others and we can become more accepting, more tolerant and more open. The I-Ching, the 300-year-old Chinese book of philosophy, maintains that once an individual has looked honestly into his own heart he will never fear any heart that comes from outside himself.

If we are to find ways to nurture peace in ourselves, then we must make room for silence. Silence is the beginning of peace. It is in silence we learn that there is a wisdom wider and deeper than what we know. In silence we can enter the rawness and poverty of our own humanity and see the whole world within us. It is in times of quiet, when we are alone with ourselves and our God, that inner peace can grow and spread so that it fills our hearts.

facing our own violence

It is only when we confront the conflict, the violence and the anger in ourselves that we can truly know ourselves, and it is only when we truly know ourselves that we can be truly at peace with ourselves. We can only become peace-filled people if we first acknowledge our own propensity to violence and conflict and learn from it.

When I was younger, I was a victim of my own anger and self-righteousness, and it was only when I took time to examine what was happening in my own heart and how much my resolve to 'put things right' was driving me on, that I began to see how much unrest I had within myself. My inner life, I realised, was a microcosm of the world, being fuelled by anger and self-righteousness.

I spent time in prayer and in discussion with Peter Birch (the late Bishop of Ossory and a personal friend and mentor) and the well-known Christian worker on behalf of the marginalised and the disabled, Jean Vanier, who is also a friend and mentor. With their help, and with the help of my constant reading of the world's great activists for peace and justice – Gandhi, Martin Luther King, Thich Nhat Hahn, Jesus – I began to realise how destructive my anger was. This process led me to acknowledge and accept my own violence and my own demons and eventually led me to peace of heart. And that inner peace has held me in the midst of all my activities on behalf of peace and justice.

This does not mean that I am not still angry at times. Of course I feel angry when I think about the fact that two billion people do not have safe drinking water in the world today; when I think how hundreds of millions of the world's people are hungry; when I realise that in every city in the world there are children being bought, sold, prostituted, abused, rejected, neglected and made homeless; when I allow myself to know that in any night in my own city of Dublin there are children homeless on the street and that 25% of the population of Ireland is living below the poverty line, and yet Ireland is ranked consistently in the higher echelons of successful, competitive countries in the world; when I think about the people all over the world who are hidden away in ghettos, poverty-stricken in the midst of plenty; when I think about the old people and people with disabilities who are hidden and forgotten in homes and institutions in our so-called developed societies; when I am reminded that in every part of the world there are people at war, people being killed for unjust reasons, and when I remember how much we in the developed part of the world exploit the poorer nations.

Injustices like these make me angry, of course they do, but I realise now that it is how I deal with that anger and continue to work for peace and justice that is important. I find that it is in reflection and prayer and silence that I can turn my anger into courage and hope and a peace-filled approach to action.

working for peace and justice

It is a contradiction in terms to fight for peace and justice. Workers for peace and justice like Dorothy Day and Martin Luther King understood this. People of peace and justice need to discover ways to work for peace and justice that are not about fighting; they need to discover a way to oppose and still be beyond opposition; they need to discover a way to express their points while remaining outside the destructive clash of opinion; they need to find a way to call for justice without being self-righteous or judgemental.

We all know that we are supposed to love our enemy. Another way of phrasing that is to say we should be in harmony with our opponents. That seems impossible, yet if we are in harmony with ourselves, we can learn to be in harmony with the movement of the whole universe and to step back and see the total picture with a perspective that is spacious. That is the way to become people of peace and justice.

That is how Gandhi operated. At one point in his campaign for the independence of the Indian people, his supporters did not know what action to take next, so Gandhi went off by himself to be quiet and to listen. He listened for three months, much to the impatience of his supporters, and then he set off on the 'salt march'.

In his listening he had heard how close salt was to the daily lives of the people, how it came from the sea itself, nature's provision, and yet it was taxed by the British. He heard that the masses could be moved by so simple a gesture as claiming the salt of God's sea. He heard that the British were vulnerable. Public opinion at home was turning, labour unions were already sympathetic to the struggle. He heard that if he set out, people would join him – that all he had to do was to start walking.

And people did join him. More and more people followed him and when they arrived at the sea, Gandhi bathed and purified himself and took a handful of salt from the beach and just held it up. Within one month seventy thousand people were jailed for mining their own salt and more were to follow their example. This was clearly ridiculous: Gandhi knew that there would be nothing for the British to do except back down, and so they did.

Gandhi knew in the silence of his heart the right action to take at the right time. He also knew that whatever was done for peace and justice had to be done in the spirit of peace and justice. Gandhi knew that freedom had to be freedom for the oppressor and the oppressed alike. 'The British must leave as friends,' he said.

Martin Luther King thought along similar lines:

> *The non-violent approach does not immediately change the heart of the oppressor; it first does something to the hearts and souls of those committed to it. It gives them a new self-respect. It calls on sources of strength and courage that they did not know they had. Finally it reaches the opponent and so stirs his consciousness that reconciliation becomes a reality.*

The question for all of us working for peace and justice is: What are we seeking and how are we seeking it and are they in harmony? In other words, our work for peace and justice should be driven by peace and justice themselves, not by anger and self-righteousness. People who are truly working for peace and justice would be uncomfortable if somebody else is diminished or defeated in the course of our actions for peace and justice. Otherwise, what we are doing is out of harmony with what we are trying to achieve.

freedom

Peace and justice are not some final tactic, a way to tie up loose strings. Peace and justice are not a treaty signed between heads of state. Peace and justice are not about winning or losing; peace and justice are about freedom. Peace and justice are a continuous state of consciousness.

What Gandhi had in mind throughout his work was to free both the colonised and the colonials. What Martin Luther King had in mind throughout the Civil Rights Movement was to liberate everyone in the US from the curse of racism, not just the black people. What José Eduardo Umana, the highly respected Colombian human rights activist and professor of criminal law, had in mind in his tireless work for the people of Colombia was an end to discrimination and the bringing about of civil rights for everyone; he was shot dead in his modest home in Bogota for taking the stand he took.

What John Hume had in mind for the people of Northern Ireland was to rid Northern Ireland of the scourge of conflict and strife. He worked for thirty years, suffering calumny from republicans, unionists, loyalists and the media, and as he worked people were being killed almost daily. Yet even when he seemed exhausted and others had walked away, he remained steadfastly a man of and for peace. He never flinched, believing that he was going to see the day when there would be peace, and this belief led to the Good Friday Agreement in 1998.

our common humanity

The only way it seems possible to achieve the extraordinarily difficult goals those people set themselves, and to achieve our own goals for peace and justice, is to remember who we are. Behind all our conflicts, our differences, our disagreements, ugly and brutal and violent though they often are, we have to hold on to the idea that we are all human; even with deep differences, we are all God's children, and that means that we are all essentially one. This essential truth of our common humanity needs to be deep in us, so that it can be revealed and come to the light even in the midst of the most terrible conflict, and so that it can make its way into horrific situations, where we least expect to find it.

Anyone who chooses to enter the arena of peace and justice must have a deep desire for unity, a desire that is profound and inclusive and that goes deep within us to the place where we are all one and that it is strong enough to stay steadfast and alive even under the worst of circumstances.

When our desire for peace and justice is strong and durable it flows over into peace and justice around us and we take it with us wherever we go. It becomes our practice. We are here with and for peace and justice and that is visible in everything we say and do. As we meet, as we plan, as we speak and as we march, peace and justice are at the heart of it.

A TIME TO LAUGH

One should take good care not to grow too wise for so great a pleasure of life as laughter.

JOSEPH ADDISON

Laughter is always a grace. It is music to the soul. It raises the heart and spirit and refreshes the body and when it comes into our lives nothing is too difficult, nothing can defeat us. We can survive almost anything when we have the gift of laughter. Life has its ups and downs, but laughter helps to make the down parts endurable. When we laugh, life is good and goodness is all around us and that makes us more gentle with ourselves and with others.

Jung had a consuming fascination with the importance of play in our lives as an opportunity to enable us to be free to make decisions, to escape from projects and pressures, expectations and protocol. Charlie Chaplin wrote, 'Laughter is the tonic, the relief, the surcease for pain.' He must have laughed when he entered a Charlie Chaplin look-a-like contest in Monte Carlo and the judges decided to give him third place!

laughing at ourselves

Laughter gives us the freedom to believe in things that other people would regard as foolish and impossible. Laughter is a healthy business, but it is especially good for our hearts and souls when we are able to laugh at ourselves. It is time to laugh when our best plans fail and the world doesn't fall asunder. It is time to laugh when we make a terrible *faux pas* that everyone notices except ourselves and nobody gets hurt.

During Churchill's last year in office while he was attending an official ceremony he heard people whispering behind him: 'That's Winston Churchill. They say he's going senile. They say he should step aside and leave the running of the nation to more dynamic and capable men.' When the ceremony was finished, Churchill turned around and said, 'Gentlemen, they also say he's deaf.'

Churchill was poking fun at the whisperers, but his humorous response also shows an unusual ability not to take himself too seriously. Likewise, Oscar Wilde, when somebody asked him what he thought about the bad review one of his plays had got, was able to joke about it: 'The play was wonderful, but the audience were terrible.' He refused to take the bad review too seriously, to get either hurt and withdrawn or pompous and nasty about it: instead, he made fun, if not exactly of himself, certainly of the situation.

It is always time to laugh at ourselves. When we take a good look at ourselves in the mirror or get a glimpse of ourselves in a shop window looking as if we carried the cares of the world on our shoulders, we should be able to laugh at what we see. When we laugh at our mistakes we can see the irrelevance of the things that worry us, and we learn to distinguish between what is important and what is not.

When we find ourselves in situations that are out of our control, laughter is often the best response, because there is nothing we can do about it anyway. That's what I had to do on the day I found myself wearing two different coloured shoes when I went to visit a government minister – there was nothing I could do about it so I could only laugh, and anyway it *was* funny. It is good to laugh when things don't work out for us, when we find ourselves at the wrong movie because we went in the wrong door of the cinema, or when we arrive at the wrong place at the right time or the right place at the wrong time for an interview or appointment. Above all, we should know how to laugh at ourselves when we creep up on ourselves and find that we are playing God. When we take things too seriously and people laugh at us, it is better to laugh with them rather than get angry or embarrassed.

humourless people

There are some people who are without a sense of humour altogether. Maybe they never had it or maybe they think they don't need it. Maybe they are afraid that they will not be taken seriously if they are able to laugh.

Children laugh at the smallest little things. They are full of fun. Unfortunately, we adults drive it out of them. 'Stop laughing,' we say, 'Take that smirk off your face,' 'Grow up,' 'Settle down.' Laughter is often represented to children as immaturity. People without a sense of humour may perhaps be people who took that message too seriously when they were children and grew up thinking that laughter was silly or irreverent or immature.

It's often very hard-working, intense people who do not see the lighter side of life and who cannot stand a sense of humour in anyone else. But working without ceasing in the interest of success and achievement can drain the life from us. Seeing nothing as a source of laughter can eat into our souls, and it makes people much more difficult to live and work with.

Sometimes people's lack of a sense of humour is due to a negativity in their whole approach to life. There is an Irish word, *cnáimhsealaí*, that is used to describe people who are the carriers of the wrath of God, of doom and gloom. They see no joy in the pursuit of goodness or wholeness. They believe laughter diminishes or takes from the sacredness of life, whereas on the contrary it adds to it.

appropriate laughter

Goethe wrote that 'People show their character in nothing more clearly than in what they think laughable.' Prayer and churches and religion are particularly considered serious business, which of course they are, but we were not taught as children that spirituality is light, joyful, happy, and that laughter can be an appropriate spiritual response. In the Old Testament, Sarah (Abraham's wife) laughed when she was told that she was pregnant at the age of eighty and I'm sure God did too.

Most things in life can be laughable; nevertheless there are experiences that do not call for laughter such as sorrow, loss or bereavement. Neither are jokes that reinforce racism, sexism or ageism or any form of oppression laughable, because they do not raise the spirit or refresh the human heart. Poking fun at people's disabilities is often disguised as humour, but it diminishes rather than uplifts humanity and is really not funny.

laughter and pain

We all know how close laughter and tears are. The eastern poet and mystic Kahlil Gibran puts it like this: 'The self-same well from which your laughter rises was oftentimes filled with tears.' We often find tears rolling down our faces when we laugh and we sometimes feel a desperate need to giggle even when we are on the edge of tears. Even our facial expressions are similar when we are laughing and crying.

It's important to cry when we are in pain, when we have suffered a loss or are grieving. It is the primary way that we can release tension under pressure, and if we suppress it we only increase that tension and stress. So we need to make room for crying in our lives, for our physical and mental well-being. 'Those who do not know how to weep with their whole heart,' said Golda Meir, the late Israeli Prime Minister, 'don't know how to laugh.' But continuous crying is not healthy either. We must at some time put what we are crying about into context and perspective so we can get on with our lives. Tears cannot do that but humour can. Laughter helps us to transcend our suffering, whereas crying does not. Tears of sadness can turn us inward, into ourselves, whereas laughter turns us outward, giving us a sense of context and proportion, a new way of seeing things.

When we are open to life, when we can allow things to happen without trying to push them away or force them, then we are able to laugh. The Buddhist teacher Stephen Levine, who spent most of his life working with people who are dying, stresses over and over again the importance of 'allowing an openness to the absurdity of the moment'. With an openness like this, we can laugh and laugh again after even the most painful experiences.

Laughter makes the seriousness of life bearable. It brings a certain transparency and it helps us to see life in context. But it may take time to be able to laugh again when we have been sad. Mark Twain said that people who overstay their welcome cannot just be thrown out the window but must be coaxed a step at a time towards the door. This is how we have to deal with our pain too, coaxing it out the door with our humour and our lightness.

Humour is the best medium for reducing stress. It promotes physical healing and is essential for mental health. In their book, *Grist for the Mill,* Stephen Levine and Ram Dass tell a story about a workshop taken by a young woman in her twenties who was dying of cancer. She asked her participants what they would feel if they were visiting a young 25-year-old mother who was dying of cancer. They replied that they would feel sad, frightened, confused, angry, pity and sympathy. Then she asked them how they would feel if they were 25 and dying of cancer and all their visitors felt like that. Through this exercise, she was able to help the people in the workshop to realise that the most important gifts people who are around the dying can bring are joy, hope and good humour. Laughter is never more necessary than in the face of death.

Eliot's joke

We usually imagine T S Eliot as a rather grave and intense person. However, Donald Hall recalls asking him for some advice when he was a young poet, about to leave Harvard and go to Oxford, knowing that Eliot had made the same transition in his own life, many years earlier. Eliot agreed that he had some advice for him. With bated breath, Hall waited for the words of wisdom that would fall from the lips of the revered elder poet. 'I waited,' he said, 'for the words I would repeat for the rest of my life, from the elder to the younger, setting me on the road of emulation.' Then, after due pause and with a comedian's sense of timing, Eliot finally spoke: 'Have you long underwear?' he asked.

A TIME TO SEARCH

The alternative to a changed society is darkness.

ERIC HOBSBAWM

Over the past century it has become possible for us to exert an unprecedented influence on nature. We can control the dark with electricity and bacteria with antibiotics. What science has made possible today would have been unthinkable even twenty years ago. Now we can apply external solutions to what we would have had to come to terms with in the past.

In the past, we had to accept the forces that we could not change or control. Our parents and grandparents accepted easily that there is much that is beyond the capacity of our human or rational minds, and that left room for their belief in a supreme being. It left room for faith in a higher power. It left room for God. Today, on the other hand, we live in a world of expanding choices, of enormous freedom, of great potential and of increasing human control over the environment; all this tends to lead us to believe that we can go it alone, we can do it by ourselves.

Where in the past faith gave meaning and peace to our lives, today consumerism has stepped in. In the past we accepted the trials and sufferings of the day and the unpredictability of the future as given. Now everything is designed to prevent or postpone discomfort, and we are encouraged to add more things to our lives to give us happiness. So we work to get the second car and the second holiday, the en-suite bathrooms, the extra televisions and videos and gadgets, the designer labels and brand names – all of which are portrayed as essential to our lives and wellbeing. We are led to believe that there is no problem that cannot be relieved, temporarily at least. Everything in our world tells us that the solution we are waiting for can be found in things.

addiction to work

And the way to acquire things, we are taught, is to work. Over the past twenty years, working hours have gone up in the United States by the equivalent of one extra month a year, and vacation time is down by 3.5 days a year. The Japanese now work 400 hours a year more than most Europeans – that is equivalent to an extra ten working weeks – and take less than eight days a year of paid holidays. In fact, they even have a word to describe death from overwork – *karoshy*. According to Charles Handy, half of them live in fear of such a death.

It is very easy to get caught up in an addiction to work. Many of us are under pressure in the workplace, with deadlines to meet and competitors chasing up close behind us if we stop to draw breath. Then there is the pressure we put on each other at work, with one person setting the pace and other people feeling they have to keep up.

The urge to work is seductive. Irresistible voices tell us, 'Work hard and you will be rewarded,' 'You deserve to have the best, to have everything, if you work for it.' We have learned to believe that if we could only be good enough, work hard enough, get it right, we could get control over our work and our life and make it turn out the way we want it. We live on the edge, tantalisingly close to having it all. Just another bit of work, another bit of effort, another bit of time, another bit of energy and we will have it all. So we work as hard as we can, and life becomes a struggle; yet the longed-for moment when we have control of our lives and everything we want never arrives.

We all have to work, of course (if we are lucky enough to have jobs), and working means having to come up to other people's expectations and having to accommodate other people's plans, which in turn means having to meet our deadlines. We can't just pretend these pressures don't exist. But like most things in life it is a question of balance. We need to be able to find a balance in our lives between work and play, between the demands of other people and our own needs, between activity and tranquillity, between the urban and the rural, between work, prayer and recreation, between night and day, between speed and rest – a balance in time and space.

In every workplace I have worked in over the past thirty years, I have tried to create a quiet room, a space set aside where the people working in the organisation could be silent with themselves from time to time, could take an opportunity to re-collect themselves at times during busy days. Some people I have worked with have been glad of these little quiet spaces in a busy day, and it has been amazing how much use the quiet rooms have got; but it is equally amazing how other people have tried to claim the quiet space for another use, for themselves and their activities. This is not to criticise: it is simply that we are all under so much pressure, especially in the workplace, pressures of time and space, that we can easily get caught in a tug-of-war of competing needs.

things we cannot control

Sooner or later we all realise that there are some things we simply cannot have, no matter how hard we work for them, and that there are some things that we simply cannot control, no matter how hard we try. It may be a sudden death that brings this home to us, or an illness, an accident, a job loss, a wrong judgement, a marital problem, a child on drugs. Whatever it is, we all come up against something in life that cannot be controlled.

Even a major problem, though, may not stop us in our tracks; we may still continue to struggle to be in control and stay so busy that we do not even give ourselves time to admit that all is not well, that we are not happy, that we are not contented, that we are not at peace, that we are running scared – scared of losing our job, our business, our clients, our health, our spouse, our children. If we reach that point in our lives we are operating out of fear, and very quickly we lose our creativity and our vitality. We even lose our perspective, our authenticity, our insightfulness and our inspiration, because all our energies are being used to keep things under control. Operating out of fear is exhausting.

When we deny that we cannot control everything and deny our spiritual needs and the yearning spirit within us which cannot be satisfied with things, there is a danger that we will turn against ourselves, blame ourselves, get angry with ourselves for our restlessness of soul and our spiritual hunger. So we continue to deny and to blot out what we know deep within our consciousness and we continue to try for greater success. If we continue to deny our inner yearning and the spirit within, we may live our whole lives at the mercy of a competitive, consumer-driven world.

glimpses of the spirit

It is when we stop and face the fact that the struggle is inside ourselves and with ourselves that we can begin to see how the theory of control we have accepted in the past is flawed and that we cannot, after all, control everything. Then we begin to get glimpses of a different reality and of a part of ourselves that we have neglected, that we have not tended to, that we have denied. That part is our spirit, which can never be satisfied with things. Charles Handy writes, in his extraordinary book *The Hungry Spirit,* 'Belief begins when facts run out': in other words, it is when we abandon our notion that we can understand and know and control our world through science and technology and facts that we can find space in our lives for faith.

When we relinquish the idea that we can be eternally in control and recognise our spiritual nature, questions present themselves to us about the meaning of life. This experience will be different for everyone, and it may begin to dawn on each of us for different reasons. How we handle this experience will be different for us all too, depending on our circumstances. Some people may turn to a consultant, a psychotherapist or a counsellor; some may turn back to a church that they have left or a belief system that they have abandoned earlier in life; others may seek a new belief system or join an alternative church.

facing ourselves

Any of these may help us to touch into our inner spirit; or none of them may. What is all-important at a time when we are searching for meaning, regardless of how we go about our search, is that we are able to admit that we cannot control everything, and that we are able to admit our pain and our hunger for something deeper in our lives. What is important is that we find it within us to sit patiently with the complexity of life, with our broken, fragile world and with the imperfections and frailty of our own lives; facing the fact that we can never be good enough to fix everything that happens to us; facing the fact that the possibility of living a deeper and fuller life may elude us again; accepting that – just as we all have physical needs for food, shelter and sleep – we have spiritual needs that need to be fulfilled.

The first step towards living a deeper, fuller life is not to deny our pain, our fragility, our inability to control, the fragility of the world, of the earth, and of the starving spirit within us. Some people may have the courage to take that risk early on; others may not have this courage until they have exhausted every possible alternative. And it *is* a risk, because we abandon our illusion of control in order to escape the destructive forces of achievement, success, consumerism and self-obsession; it is a risk in this rational, controlling world to abandon ourselves to something beyond our control; it is a risk because we are afraid that we will lose ourselves in the process; it is a risk because we are afraid that we will be let down if we take a leap of faith for a life that has meaning.

Yet it is only by taking that risk that we can find inner peace, it is only by taking that leap that we can start our inner journey of fulfilment and happiness. This journey we start by letting go of our desire to control will lead us to a happiness and fulfilment that can never come from things, a happiness that is much deeper and much more pervasive and much more evident to the people around us.

interconnections

Deep within us we all know that we cannot escape from our dependence on other people and our connectedness with the world. 'All life is an interconnected membrane,' says Annie Dillard, 'a weft of linkages like a chain mail', or as my old friend Peig Sayers says, 'Is ar scath a chéile a mhaireann na daoine' (people live in each other's shadow). Whether we are conscious of it or not, what is happening right around the world has implications for who we are, what we are and what we are doing. Our words, our actions, our movements have worldwide reverberations.

There are people in parts of the world so poor that they over-cultivate and fertilise their land, cut their trees down because they cannot afford any other fuel or burn their animals' dung rather than use it as manure. There are people whose topsoil is being washed away so that they are left with a desert or hard, burnt mud. These things are happening in Africa or Asia or South America, but that doesn't mean it has nothing to do with us in the West. On the contrary, all this is happening because of decisions and actions taken by the rest of us in the richer parts of the world.

Millions of people die of starvation each year; one-third of the world's workers are unemployed or underemployed; 70% of world trade is managed by 400 corporations; in the US in 1989 1% of the population earned over a half a million dollars per person per year, more than the whole 40% of the population at the bottom earned between them; in the UK in 1996, when it boasted the fastest-growing economy in the EU, 17.2% were living below the poverty line; in Ireland today, where we claim to be the eleventh most economically competitive country in the world, we have between 20% and 25% of our population living below the poverty line. These things concern us all. Whether we are conscious of it or not we all carry responsibility for the good and the evil in our world today. Even the most apparently insignificant action, once started, will echo into immeasurable distances.

community

Deep down in the heart of each of us is the desire to be ourselves, to become what we are capable of. Equally deep is the desire to find a purpose bigger than ourselves, because we know it will make us better people, bigger people, much more than we can ever dream of on our own. Everyone's journey to find that purpose is different, yet many people have made the journey before us. Many people in our time are already on that journey and if we look around us with our eyes and hearts open we will find people who are on this journey whom we may not have noticed before. These are the prophetic people of our time, who are calling us forth from the delusion of the rational world of the twenty-first century.

Prophetic people in today's world often live and work in community. A community is any group of people with something in common and living or working together, either formally or informally; but I am using the word here, in a slightly specialised sense, to mean people with shared interests and values who purposely choose to live or work together for some reason to do with those values. Examples of such communities with a Christian spiritual basis are L'Arche, Genesis, ATD Fourth World, Sojourners, Jerusalem Community, Camphill, Loaves and Fishes, Jesuit Community of Volunteers, Focus Community Service Volunteers, Emmaus, Sanctuary; there are also numerous Buddhist communities like this and many other communities of peace and reconciliation, with other religious affiliations or with none, all over the world.

Some people are forming communities like these within their own neighbourhood or parish; others are travelling hundreds of miles to join communities of faith, justice and service. Being in community does not necessarily mean living together (although it often does). Members of communities like this may live in different places, but they are in constant communication with each other, affirming and supporting each other.

Communities like this are about building up anew the broken humanity of the world, building up the lives of people who are sick and dying, aged and oppressed, people who are disabled and homeless, people who are refugees and prisoners, people who are apathetic and indifferent, people who are unemployed and abandoned, people who are mentally ill and lonely, people who are fearful and unloved, people who are at war with each other. These community-builders, by using their qualities of intuition, creativity, compassion, justice and love, are co-creators of reconciliation for individuals, families and society. Attentive to the cry of the poor, the oppressed and the marginalised, they work to break the shell of injustice, prejudice and fear that protects societies and limits their vision. They are people of peace who work for the reconciliation of the oppressor and the oppressed, to build in their way, in their place, a world of love, peace and justice. They are remaking and reshaping the social fabric, whether that is at the level of home, street, neighbourhood, small caring groups or city. They are trying to create an atmosphere of freedom and acceptance where people can sit together, friend and foe, oppressor and oppressed, givers and receivers and choose to change and be reconciled.

stanhope green

I am a member of a religious order or community called the Sisters of Charity. For years, I lived in a convent, with other members of my community. In the 1990s, I began to live, with two other sisters, as part of the community of Focus Ireland at Stanhope Green in the inner city of Dublin. Stanhope Green is at one level a housing development, providing living accommodation for people who would otherwise be homeless. At another level, we are a community of people with a wide range of potentials and needs, people who are sick and well, able and disabled. We all share a single space and time. We meet, touch, embrace and learn more about each other daily, giving and taking life. We share a sacred space – a sanctuary and sanctuary garden – where we replenish our minds and hearts and spirit, all the time learning more about the uncertainties, consistencies and ambiguities of our lives. Learning more about the distance between what we are and what we say, learning more about the great poverty and brokenness of our own lives, we are also learning more about our potential and strength and the source of it.

Here in Stanhope Green we have come to appreciate the great potential of community. We have learned that community cannot be defined too narrowly or too literally; and it is never static, but always dynamic. We have learned too that community is much wider than the core community of Stanhope Green. Our life is lived also in communion with the many small gatherings of people across the world united across divides of race, sex, culture, age, creed and status. We have learned that if we are to be a challenging and inspiring community we must move outside ourselves to work with other communities right across the city, the country and the world.

I have learned that for a community to work takes effort, it takes time and it takes commitment. Its growth and evolution depends on the efforts and commitment of each of us. I have come to realise what St Paul meant when he advised the Galatians 'bear one another's burdens': he meant to respect each other and above all other's freedom, each other's gifts and each other's individuality. This means accepting also each other's oddities, idiosyncrasies and weaknesses and accepting and acknowledging and facing everything that produces friction or conflict amongst us. In bearing each other's burdens we know that our burdens too are being borne, and that is our greatest source of strength.

We exist in relation to each other but continue to develop our own identity, recognising that the community has the right to expect, suggest and require certain things from us and we continue to seek a balance between our own personal identity and integrity and fidelity to community. I have learned that each community needs a vision and it is that vision that brings people together and it is that vision that binds us in strength and in hope. Our vision in Stanhope Green is to give and receive, recognising the gifts and the frailty of each of us as a continuous source of challenge, renewal and bonding, as we return to it again and again in reflection, prayer and sharing, to discover what God is calling us to now. We have discovered too that while companioning is essential to community, the true test of our unity is the service we offer daily in lives of compassion.

We have discovered the importance of silence and solitude. We have learned how to be alone within the community. We have learned that our deepest self is born in silence and the individual wisdom of our innermost being is replenished in silence. These are the gifts we bring and offer to our community, and these are the gifts we receive in community. Stanhope Green has helped me to begin to resolve that pull between a fast life whizzing past and the desire to slow down and to live each moment more fully.

It is in our individuality and diversity that we are made whole in community. It is as Jung said: 'I need we to be truly I.' We are each distinct and different but part of something bigger. But while each of us has our own clear identity, that identity is changed, developed and made more complete by being part of a community.

We have learned the great challenge of living close to people who are or have been oppressed or marginalised. When we live in Stanhope Green we cannot ignore the pain of our neighbours. The daily reality of inner city life is present to us all the time. Young people lonely and lost, people without homes, families broken or breaking up, troubled people with innumerable problems – all are part of our daily life. All the time we are being challenged by the loneliness, the pain, the sadness, the poverty, the oppression of the people around us.

living close to oppression

Living close to oppression opens us up to a new understanding and a new compassion. Hardness of heart cannot be maintained for long in the midst of such obvious human suffering. I have discovered and I know that it is only when my eyes have been opened and my heart softened by the poor that I am really ready to begin to work with the poor and ready to change the circumstances of their lives.

God identifies with the poor not because they are more noble but because they are more vulnerable. Those of us who are not poor are much less vulnerable. Being close to the poor helps us all to remove our hearts of stone and replace them with hearts of flesh. It helps us to see ourselves as we really are, to see our intolerance, our impatience, our attachment to security, status and privileges. It shows us our frail human nature. Above all, it forces us to search for the meaning of life and what we are called to be. This is not easy for any of us. It is a call to a radical conversion of heart for all of us.

finding inner peace

A rich young man once ran up to Jesus and asked, 'Good master, what must I do to inherit eternal life?' Today, a rich young person is more likely to ask 'How can I find meaning in my life? What is the purpose of life? I have everything and I live a reasonably honest and honourable life, but I am not contented. How can I find inner peace?' The Bible tells us quite simply that 'Jesus looked on the young man and loved him.' Then he advised him to sell all he had and give to the poor; nor did he stop there – he also said 'and come follow me.'

Jesus knew how easily we can all get trapped and be under the control of possessions, how we can be up to our necks in debt and how, even though we have everything, we are still fearful of not having enough. Jesus was sensitive to this situation, to this struggle. He invited the young man, as he invites each of us today, to follow him, to experience a new kind of security, where we will meet people like ourselves, people with the same fears, problems and history, but people who all want to learn a new way of being, to discover a new meaning in life, a new contentment and peace of heart.

Jesus is not saying to everyone literally, 'Go this minute and sell everything you have and give it to the poor.' But he is inviting us all to follow him with an open heart, assuring us that he will lead us in the way that is best for us. For some of us it is literally leaving everything to follow him; for others the challenge in following Jesus is to detach ourselves from the things that bind us to the world of speed and work and consumerism that we live in.

the challenge

The quest for meaning is not easy. It is a challenge. It can be lonely. It takes courage, because we have to let go of acceptable, conventional values and follow our own inner wisdom. We are setting ourselves apart from the comfort and support of a society with its promises and illusions. We are embarking on a journey that does not give immediate certainties or immediate rewards, but it is a challenge that we must take on if we are to find our inner peace and the greatness to which we are called. It is a challenge, but it is one that we can meet when we go into the depths of our own hearts. Václav Havel, the former president of the Czech Republic says, 'The salvation of this human world lies nowhere else than in the human heart.'

None of us can tell anyone else that our belief system is right, even though we are sure it is right for us. Faith is a very personal (though not a private) matter. Still, respecting other people's right to believe differently, I share my beliefs and my struggles because I believe that doing so may be a source of strength, hope and confidence for others who are seriously seeking a deeper meaning in their lives and who are about to take the risk to reach beyond their way of life.

It is a risk to do that, but it is only a risk until we do it. When we take that risk, make that leap, empty ourselves of the illusion of who we are and what we think we are and what we think we can control, then we find that there is less to be feared because there is less to lose than we thought.

The philosopher Schopenhauer compares life to a piece of embroidery, where we get to see the wrong side first, and then the right side. 'The wrong side is not so pretty as the right, but it is more instructive. It shows the way in which the threads have been worked together.' It is when we come to appreciate the wrong side from which we have woven our lives that we will be inspired to look, to question, to move out. But if we are not prepared to look at the wrong side and keep our gaze on the pretty side of life, with all its illusions and promises, we will not develop our capacity for awareness and inspiration. We can only develop our awareness and our inspiration when we are prepared to accept ourselves as we are.

fruitfulness

Like the young man who approached Jesus in the Bible, we all need security. There is a healthy balance between security and risk and that balance is one each of us must find for ourselves. Our own experience is the only one that is real for us. Whatever balance we decide to strike in our own lives between our need for security and our willingness to take risks, we can only be fully alive when we find the deeper meaning of our life within ourselves. We need to be open to the process, to be open to change, to be prepared to forgive ourselves for our past, to accept our limits and our possibilities and to give as much attention to our inner journey of the spirit as to our outer journey of career and achievement.

When we are too caught up with our projects and programmes, our status and our success, we can miss out on the most important things, which are about our inner self, our inner resources. As the Little Prince in the story says, the most important things are hidden. The greatest challenge of the future is to call on our inner resources as never before.

We are pioneers at the start of the third millennium, challenged to call forth the human spirit and to feed the yearning within our human hearts. The challenge of our generation is to expand our definition of success to include spiritual qualities and life experiences that run counter to the values of an achievement- and consumer-oriented society. When we begin to define success in terms of fruitfulness, we experience a different type of fulfilment, because by being fruitful we are what we are called to be. If we have replaced ambition with purpose, and if we are motivated by inspiration rather than by fear, then ultimately we will reap our fruit by working less and achieving more.

When we aspire to be fruitful there are no rights or wrongs – we simply become what we are meant to be. As we look around us, we will see the best that can be expected of any of us.

The disabled person or handicapped person can be as fruitful within their capacities in life as any of us can be, if we create a society that will enable us to be within our different capacities. It has nothing to do with apparent results; it has everything to do with who we are and what we are called to be. As the character Mr Atha says of a disabled child in Morris West's novel *The Clowns of God:* 'This little one is my sign to you. Treasure her.'

A TIME FOR HOPE

Hope has to do with believing beyond today and encourages us to follow our dreams. Hope is trusting that what is happening will eventually make sense, or if it never makes sense, it will still offer an opportunity for growth. Hope assures us each morning that our life is of value no matter how unsettling or disturbing our current situation may be. Hope nudges us when it's time to move on and encourages us not to give in. Hope accepts mystery and trusts the unknown. Hope doesn't pretend that we will get all we want or that there won't be struggle on the way, but it promises growth with the struggles.

Hope is having inner freedom in the midst of fears and weaknesses. Hope is finding the truth about ourselves in the midst of darkness. Hope is accepting our mortality when we encounter our own physical weaknesses. Hope is living our dreams even when we experience failure and self-doubt.

There is an Ethiopian legend about a shepherd boy, Alemayu. Alemayu had spent the night on a bitterly cold mountain. He had only a thin cloth to wear. To the amazement of all the villagers, he returned alive and well. When they asked him how he survived, he replied:

> *The night was bitter. And all the sky was dark, I thought I would die. Then far, far off I saw a shepherd's fire on another mountain. I kept my eyes on the red glow in the distance, and I dreamed of being warm. And that is how I had the strength to survive.*

Each of us has a 'shepherd's fire on another mountain' that has kept our hope alive. When the nights are dark and bitterly cold, we have seen something 'far, far off' that has helped us survive. This 'fire' has given us the courage to recover and to believe in the dreams that stir in our souls.

beginning again

Sam Keen opens his book *Beginnings Without End* with a brilliant story about hope. Keen tells about a dream that changed his life. In the dream, a man walked into his room. The man came over, sat on the edge of Keen's bed, and said to him: 'I have learned one important thing in life – how to begin again.'

Beginning again – with the wisdom we have acquired from experience and discovering who we have become and who we are now – is a central part of hope. This determination to begin again is something that has fascinated the poet Brendan Kennelly and his beautiful poem *Begin* was written as he watched the faces of people making their way to work in the morning on Pembroke Road.

> *Though we live in a world that dreams of ending,*
> *that always seems about to give in,*
> *something that will not acknowledge conclusion*
> *insists that we forever begin.*
>
> BRENDAN KENNELLY

Albert Camus is a great example of beginning again and of hope. For years Camus had fought against injustice because he could not deny the reality of suffering and poverty in the world. Yet he also refused to deny the great daily miracle of creation.

When he returned from France to his native Algeria at the end of the Second World War, he returned to his own village, Tifasa, a beautiful but very poor village, and he wrote 'Poverty taught me that all was not well under the sun, but the sun taught me that poverty was not everything.' Here he found a new energy; a new hope in the daily miracle of creation. He could begin again. For Camus, this beginning again is closely linked to one's capacity for admiration, to appreciate what you have not made but which is nonetheless given.

In her diaries, *An Interrupted Life*, written in Holland during the time when the Jews were being rounded up for deportation, Etty Hillesum revealed the possibility of hope, even in the darkest of times. Etty describes herself as a sophisticated although somewhat silly young woman who lived in a communal household in Amsterdam when suddenly, unaccountably, she began to feel the need to kneel in the middle of the bedroom. Feelings of overwhelming gratitude forced her on her knees. Etty saw her fellow Jews being transported to the East. She knew the fate that awaited her and yet she still noticed the Jasmine plant and the sky outside her window. She wrote:

> How exotic the Jasmine looks, so delicate and dazzling against the mud-brown walls. I can't take in how beautiful this Jasmine is, but there is no need to, it is simply enough to believe in miracles in the twentieth century... And I do, even though the lice will be eating me up in Poland before long... I am with the hungry, with the ill-treated, with the dying everyday. I am also with the Jasmine. I am with the piece of sky beyond my window. There is room for everything in a single life.

ETTY HILLESUM

Even at a time when murder was in a state of mass production, even when evil seemed most free, Etty Hillesum refused to take the beauty of the Jasmine plant for granted. Through her acts of hope she did not let herself be defined by death and destruction.

It was hope that made room for the sun in Albert Camus' life and for the jasmine in the midst of the Holocaust in Etty Hillsum's life.

hope is divine

Hope is not optimism. It is what we have when the bottom falls out of optimism. Hope is the ability to see through the false optimism of ourtime. It is the ability to see the reality of despair in the world and yet see that all is in tune with the divine purpose of creation.

In everyday life, we can hope that our work will turn out all right, that our children will thrive, that we will have a good summer and a good harvest. These are all things we can imagine. True hope is different. It goes beyond the imaginable. True hope is divine. It is the call to be what is not yet.

To hope is to experience a power and a presence that is greater than we are, and to experience it when we do not see it. One way to experience what we do not see is to draw on memory, and especially on treasured memories such as playful childhood moments. Such memories sustain prisoners in their captivity, and they can sustain us too.

Hope is stubborn. It has the ability to accept strength and weakness. It is not arrogant, neither is it modest. Hope is daring and courageous; it has the audacity to reach a hand into the darkness and come out with a handful of light. Hope is waiting with a resilience of spirit, in the certain knowledge that if we wait long enough and if we are true to ourselves, then things will make sense. Hope lives on the edge between the near and the far, between the infinite and the finite. It is believing what is not seen; it is seeing what is not visible.

St Augustine says that hope has two daughters, anger and courage. People of hope feel with the rejected ones of society – people living with oppression and violence, anguish, abuse, people who are homeless, prostituted and unemployed. We feel their pain, their hurt, their anguish, and we are righteously angry on their behalf. It is anger and courage that enable us to make happen what we want to happen in the future. They enable us to do remarkable things; they lead us to accept as our brothers and sisters the rejected people of the world; they lead us to turn upside down the hierarchical systems, the male-dominated structures, the class-conscious conventions, the mindsets, the success syndromes; and they lead us to transform, by tiny deliberate efforts, the priorities and preoccupations of our personal lives and to believe in the transformation of society, even while nothing seems to improve or change.

the good news

If we lose touch with our sources, we are in danger of losing hope. That is why it is so important to stay close to nature, to listen to how the trees and flowers, potatoes and hedges, shrubs and bulbs grow in silence. Hope is believing there is beauty and meaning in our life right up to the last moment. When we let go, hope expands.

It is easy to allow routines, the ticking of the clock and daily trivia to rule our lives. It is only when we bend our head in prayer that we give ourselves a chance to remember that we are all on a journey; we are pilgrims, nomads, in exodus, that we have the seed of God in us, and that, as Meister Eckhart says, 'The seed of God grows into God as a hazel seed grows into a hazel tree.' It is because that seed of God is within us, wanting to grow in us, that we can't settle, we can't let ourselves become too complacent.

Our capacity for hope can diminish when there is no room for miracle or mystery. Our pragmatic mindsets can become convinced that most of the situations we find ourselves in are humanly solvable problems; problems of racism, of urban decay, of crime, of mental illness, domestic and personal problems; problems of homelessness, poverty, unemployment, even problems of inter-church dialogue. In this kind of atmosphere there is no room for hope, because hope belongs to the realm of the ongoing mystery, the human endeavour to penetrate the darkness and the obscurity of the realities that surround us.

Love and truth, suffering and death are realities that we are involved in, not objective problems we confront. We are developed by them as we experience them; we are in them, not outside them; they transcend us and compel us to explore a larger world of interaction and exchange. And that is what we are called to as Christians. That is the good news. Our lives are not trivia or defined by the problems we face. We are marked by freedom. As St Paul said, 'You are a letter of Christ, written not in ink but in the spirit of the living God.'

We are summoned as Christians to a bold commitment to act in faith. It is no trivial task to give an account of the hope that is in us in the midst of overwhelming poverty, in the face of sickness, through grief and insult and loneliness, speaking forcefully and without malice, restructuring our priorities and making credible our value systems, plodding patiently through daily tasks and commitment. The call to release life and meaning from all the secret and dim events of our personal and communal histories is our challenge as Christians.

Hope is, as Dan Berrigan puts it, 'living as though the truth were true'. It is when we are told the limits of our life that we hope.

We are called to love in love's inimitable way by service and sacrifice. Our spirits may be weak, our bodies tired, but we hunger still for the good news, and in that lies our hope. Hope is believing what is not yet seen, and seeing what is not yet visible:

> *Unseen bud's infinite hidden well*
> *Under snow and ice*
> *Under the darkness*

WALT WHITMAN

BIBLIOGRAPHY

All scriptural quotations come from the Jerusalem bible.

A Time to Live

Dag Hammarskjöld, *Markings*, trans. Leif Sjoberg and WH Auden, London: Faber, 1963

Brendan Kennelly, 'A Time for Voices'; *Selected Poems*, Newcastle-upon-Tyne, Bloodaxe, 1990

A Time to Die

Meister **Eckhart**, *Breakthrough: Meister Eckhart's Creation Spirituality*, ed Matthew Fox, New York: Doubleday, 1980

Nor **Hall**, *The Moon and Virgin: Reflections on the Archetypal Feminine*, New York: Harper and Row, 1980

Stephen **Levine**, Healing into Life and Death, New York: Doubleday, 1987

Máire **Ní Chinnéide**, *Peig*, Dublin: Comhlacht Oideachas na hÉireann

Henry **Van Dyke**, *The Upward Path: Daily Inspirations from the Works of Henry Van Dyke*, Wheaton, Illinois: Harolds Shaw, 1995

A Time to Sow

Emily **Dickinson**, *Final Harvest*, ed Thomas H Johnson, Essex: Little, Brown, 1981

Frances **Hodgson Burnett**, *The Secret Garden*, Oxford: OUP, 1987

Julian of Norwich, *Revelations of Divine Love*, trans M L del Mastro, New York: Doubleday, 1977

John **Muir**, *My First Summer in Sierra*, Boston: Haughton Mifflin Press, 1917

Rainer Maria **Rilke**, *Letter to a Young Poet*, trans Stephen Mitchell, New York: Vintage Books, 1987

May **Sarton**, *Journal of a Solitude*, New York: WW Norton, 1973

Suzuki **Shunryu**, 'Zen Mind Beginners Mind' in *Formal Talks on Zen Meditation and Practice*, ed Trudy Dixon, New York: Weather Hill, 1970

Vincent **Van Gogh**, *The Letters of Vincent Van Gogh*, ed Mark Ruskill, New York: Atheneum Macmillan Publishing Co, 1963

A Time to Reap

Willa **Cather**, *O Pioneers*, Boston: Haughton Mifflin, 1913

Thomas **Merton**, *New Seeds of Contemplation*, New York: New Directions, 1981

Henry David **Thoreau**, *The Selected Journals of Henry David Thoreau*, ed Carl Bode, New York: Signet New American Library, 1967

A Time to Reverence the Earth

Edward **Abbey**, *The Journey Home: Some Words in Defense of the American West*, Dutton

Samuel **Beckett**, *Endgame*, Faber, 1964

Thomas **Berry**, *The Dream of the Earth*, San Francisco: Sierra Book Clubs, 1998

Wendell **Berry** *Farming: A Handbook*, New York: Harcourt Brace Johanovich, 1970

Kahlil **Gibran**, *The Prophet*, Alfred Knopf Inc, 1951

Patrick **Kavanagh**, 'The Ploughman', *The Complete Poems*, The Goldsmith Press, 1972

Thomas **Merton**, *Raids on the Unspeakable*, New Directions, 1965

John G. **Neihardt**, *Black Elk Speaks*, Simon and Schuster/University of Nebraska Press, 1961

Brian **Swimme**, *The Universe is a Green Dragon: Cosmic Creation Story*, Santa Fé: Bear and Co, 1984

Henry David **Thoreau**, *Natural History Essays*, Laton, Utah: Gibbs M. Smith, 1980

Henry David **Thoreau**, *The Selected Journals of Henry David Thoreau*, ed Carl Bode, New York: Signet New American Library, 1967

Alan **Watts**, *Nature, Man and Woman* Random House, 1958

A Time for Solitude

Constantine P **Cavafy** (1863–1933) translated by Rae Davlen, San Diego: Harvest Books

G K **Chesterton**, *The Collected Works*, London: Ignatious Press, 1988

Andrew **Harvey**, *The Way of Passion*, Berkeley: Frog, 1988

Hermann **Hesse**, *Siddhartha*, London: Picador

Brendan **Kennelly**, *New and Selected Poems*, Lough Crew: Gallery Books, 1976

Thomas **Merton**, *The Conjectures of a Guilty Bystander*, New York: Doubleday, 1965

Blaise **Pascal**, *Selected Readings from Blaise Pascal*, Revel Fleming, 1991

Dylan **Thomas**, 'The Force that Through the Green Fuse Drives the Flower', in *Collected Poems*, London: Dent

Gabriele **Uhlein**, *Meditations with Hildegard of Bingen*, Santa Fé: Bear and Co, 1982

A Time to Pray

E E **Cummings**, *Collected Poems*, Harper Collins

T S **Eliot**, *The Complete Poems and Plays*, London: Faber & Faber, 1963

Denise **Levertov**, 'The Avowal', and 'Psalm Fragments', *The Dream and the Sapphire*, New York: New Directions, 1997

Anthony **de Mello**, *One Minute Wisdom*, New York: Doubleday, 1986

William **Wordsworth**, *The Poems*, ed Thomas Hutchinson, Oxford: OUP, 1926

William Butler **Yeats**, 'The Lake Isle of Innisfree', *Selected Poetry*, London: Macmillan, 1962,

A Time to be Still

Rabindranath **Tagore** (trans), *Songs of Kabir*, London: Red Wheel/Weister, 2002

Coleman **Banks**, *The Soul of Rumi*, San Francisco: Harper, 2002

Etty **Hillesum**, *An Interrupted Life and Letters from Westerbrook*, Owl Books: NY, 1996.

Robert **Frost**, *The Works of Robert Frost*, London: Wordsworth, 1884

Rainer Maria **Rilke**, from *Selected Poems of Rainer Maria Rilke*, translated by Robert Blythe, Harper and Row: New York, 1981

Henry David **Thoreau**, *The Selected Journals of Henry David Thoreau*, ed Carl Bode, New York Signet New American Library: NY, 1967

Walt Whitman, *Unseen Buds*, Alice & Rollo Silver: NY, 1966

A Time for Simplicity

Holly **Roberts**, *Tao Te Ching – The Art and the Journey*, Anjeli Press Inc

A Time to Love

Kahlil **Gibran**, *The Prophet*, Alfred Knopf Inc, 1951

Ann **Lamott**, *Bird by Bird: Some Reflections on Writing and Life*, New York: Doubleday, 1994

Nelson **Mandela**, *Long Walk into Freedom*, Abacus, 1994

Ken **Wilber**, *Grace and Grit*, London: Shanbahala, 1991

Plato 'Art and Love' in *An Illustrated Anthology of Love Poetry*, Kate Farrell, London: Little, Brown, 1990

William Butler **Yeats**, 'To the Rose upon the Road of Time', *Selected Poetry*, London: Macmillan, 1962

A Time to Take a Fresh Look

E E **Cummings**, *Collected Poems*, Harper Collins

W H **Davies**, 'Leisure', *Collected Poems*, London: Jonathan Cape, 1963

Gerard Manley **Hopkins**, 'God's Grandeur' and 'The Windhover', *Poetry of Gerard Manley Hopkins*, Penguin, 1990

Cyprian **Smith**, *The Way of Paradox: Spiritual Life as Taught by*

Meister Eckhart, London: Darton, Longman, Todd, 1987

Ester **de Waal**, *A World Made Whole: Rediscovering Celtic Traditions*, Fount/Harper Collins, 1991

William **Wordsworth**, 'Surprised by Joy', *The Poems*, ed Thomas Hutchinson, Oxford: OUP, 1926

A Time for Gratitude

Robert **Frost**, *The Works of Robert Frost*, London: Wordsworth, 1884

Rainer Maria **Rilke**, from *Selected Poems of Rainer Maria Rilke*, translated by Robert Blythe, Harper and Row: New York, 1981

Dag **Hammarskjöld**, *Markings*, trans. Leif Sjoberg and W H Auden, London: Faber, 1963

A Time to Forgive

C S **Lewis**, *Mere Christianity*, New York: Macmillan, 1996

Dag **Hammarskjöld**, *Markings*, trans. Leif Sjoberg and W H Auden, London: Faber, 1963

Scott King **Coretto**, *The Words of Martin Luther King*, New York: New Market Press, 1992

A Time to Heal

Ram **Dass** and Paul **Gorman**, *How Can I Help?* New York: Alfred A. Knopf, 1985

Marlo **Morgan**, *The Mutant Message*, Missouri: MM Co, 1991

Nancy **Wood**, *Dancing Moons*, New York: Doubleday, 1995

A Time to Come Home

Charles **Dickens**, *Nicholas Nickleby*, Penguin, 1994

T S **Eliot**, *The Four Quartets* London: Faber & Faber, 1940

Theodor **Zeldin**, *An Intimate History of Humanity*, London: Sinclair Stevenson, 1994

A Time for a Little Light

Dorothy **Day**, *The Long Loneliness*, New York: New Directions, 1975

T S **Eliot**, *Four Quartets*, London: Faber & Faber, 1940

Rabindranath **Tagore**, *Gitanjali: A Collection of Indian Songs*, New York: Macmillan Co, 1971

Jean **Vanier**, *Community and Growth*, London: Darton, Longman, Todd, 1979

Simone **Weil**, *The Simone Weil Reader*, New York: David McKay, 1977

A Time for Peace and Justice

Scott King **Coretto**, *The Words of Martin Luther King*, New York: New Market Press, 1992

Stirer, *Gandhi*, Prentice Hall, 1986

Thich **Nhat Hanh**, *Peace is Every Step*, London: Bantam Books, 1991

Thich **Nhat Hanh**, *Living Buddha, Living Christ*, London: Ryder, 1995

A Time to Laugh

Joseph **Addison,** in *Serenity*, Celia Haddon, London: Hodder and Stoughton, 1998

C J **Jung**, *The Undiscovered Self,* New York: Mentor Books, 1977

Stephen **Levine**, *Who Dies,* New York: Doubleday, 1982

Stephen **Levine** and Ram **Dass**, *Grist for the Mill,* New York: Doubleday, 1977

A Time to Search

Anne **Dillard**, *Teaching a Stone to Talk,* New York: Harper Row, 1982

Charles **Handy**, *The Hungry Spirit,* London: Random House, 1997

Charles **Handy**, *Beyond Certainty,* London: Arrow Books, 1995

Václev **Havel**, *Summer Meditations,* New York: A Knopf, 1992

Eric **Hobsbawm**, *The Age of Extremes,* Abacus, 1993

C J **Jung**, *The Undiscovered Self,* New York: Mentor Books, 1977

Máire **Ní Chinnéide**, *Peig,* Dublin: Comhlacht Oideachais na hÉireann

Antoine **de Saint Exupéry**, *The Little Prince,* Harcourt Brace Johanovich, 1971

Morris **West**, *The Clowns of God,* St Martin's Press, 1991

A Time For Hope

Brendan **Kennelly**, from *Familiar Strangers: New and Selected Poems 1960–2004,* Blood Axe Books Ltd, London: 2004

Sam **Keen**, *Beginnings Without End,* Harper & Row: NY, 1975

Etty **Hillesum**, *An Interrupted Life and Letters from Westerbrook,* Owl Books: NY, 1996.

Dan **Berrigan**, *The Word Made Fresh,* London: Orbis, 2004

Other editions of books by Sr Stan

'Even the most convinced cynics will find something in
Sister Stan's basic premise: "Take time to live - it's what life is
for." ... A work of spiritual insight.' *Ireland on Sunday*

ISBN: 1-86059-087-X
Hardback

Gardening the Soul
A spiritual daybook through the seasons
Sister Stanislaus Kennedy

'Her reflections on the balance of living and the eternal
verities are much more accessible and understandable to those
of us in the mixed-up society of today than the standard style
of the contemplative or professional retreat-giver. It is a lovely
little book.' *Books Ireland*

ISBN: 1-903650-05-4
Hardback

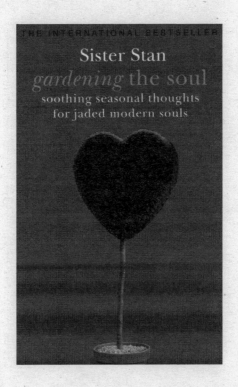

THE INTERNATIONAL BESTSELLER

Sister Stan

gardening the soul

soothing seasonal thoughts
for jaded modern souls

Soothing seasonal thoughts for jaded modern souls.

ISBN: 1-90365-058-5
Paperback

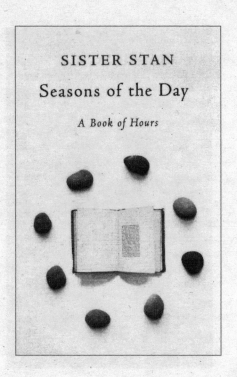

SISTER STAN

Seasons of the Day

A Book of Hours

Based on the traditional Book of Hours – psalms said daily,
at set times, by religious communities throughout the world –
Seasons of the Day reveals the enduring relevance of this
ancient practice to contemporary living.

ISBN: 1-86059-179-5
Hardback

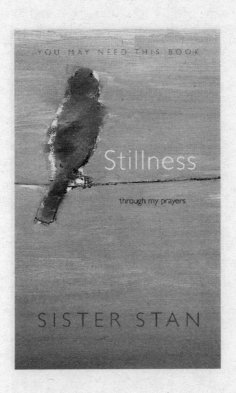

YOU MAY NEED THIS BOOK

Stillness

through my prayers

SISTER STAN

Stillness: A deep silence and quiet calm, bringing feelings of
peace, solace, contentment and serenity.

ISBN: 1-86059-251-1 /
978-1-86-059251-5
Hardback